Scenography

Scenography

Simon Donger

THE CROWOOD PRESS

First published in 2018 by
The Crowood Press Ltd
Ramsbury, Marlborough
Wiltshire SN8 2HR

www.crowood.com

© Simon Donger 2018

All rights reserved. No part of this publication may be reproduced or transmitted in any form or by any means, electronic or mechanical, including photocopy, recording, or any information storage and retrieval system, without permission in writing from the publishers.

British Library Cataloguing-in-Publication Data
A catalogue record for this book is available from the British Library.

ISBN 978 1 78500 453 7

Frontispiece
On Lies by Francesc Serra Vila. PATRICK BALDWIN

Typeset and designed by Guy Croton Publishing Services, West Malling, Kent

Printed and bound in India by Replika Press Pvt Ltd

ACKNOWLEDGEMENTS

I am forever grateful to those who have been instrumental in my scenographic education, namely: Trish Lyons, Ana Cappelluto, Chris White, and Romeo and Claudia Castellucci.

I am filled with gratitude towards the artists who have so generously and patiently contributed to this book.

Finally, I must thank the various individuals who, over the years, have inspired and supported my endeavours to promote and celebrate scenography: Joanna Parker, Madaleine Trigg, Simon Shepherd, Andrea Cusumano and Eve Katsouraki.

PHOTOGRAPHY CREDITS

Most of the photographs in the book depict the works produced by students on the scenography courses at The Royal Central School of Speech and Drama, University of London. All photography is taken by the artists named in the captions or writing the texts in which the photograph is included, unless otherwise stated in the caption.

CONTENTS

	INTRODUCTION	7
	Professional Insight: Dramaturging by Henny Dörr	
1	DRAWING	11
	Professional Insight: Listening by Dan Scott	
2	MODELLING	33
	Professional Insight: Model-Making by Yoon Bae	
3	PROTOTYPING	67
	Professional Insight: Siting by Sophie Jump	
4	COMPOSING	87
	Professional Insight: Spectating by Michael Pavelka	
5	DOCUMENTING	109
	Professional Insight: Photographing by Jemima Yong	
6	RESEARCHING	129
	Professional Insight: Measuring by Oren Sagiv	
	CONCLUSION	155
	BIBLIOGRAPHY	157
	INDEX	158

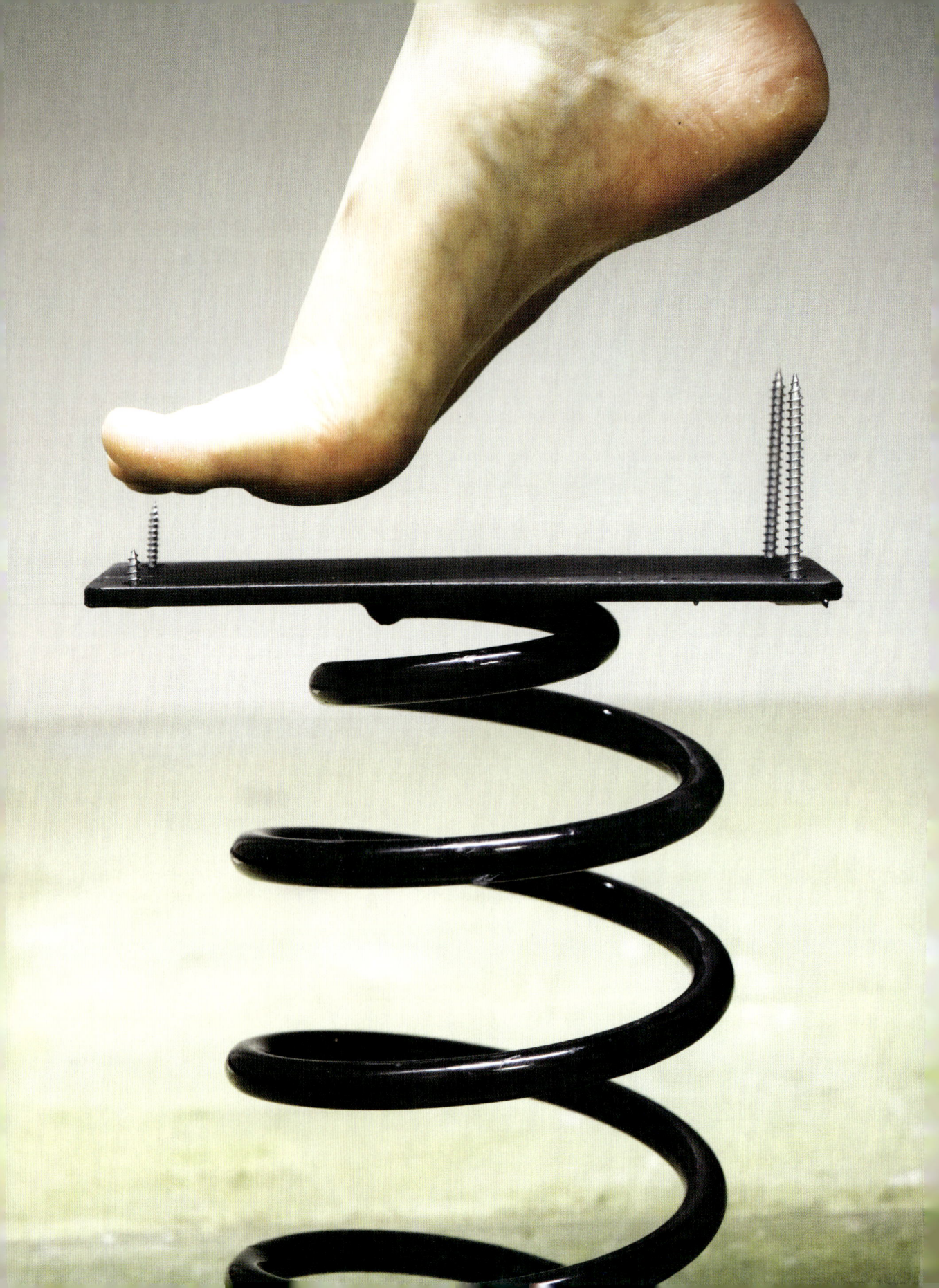

INTRODUCTION

Based on principles and processes originating in performance design, scenography is a creative framework for the conception of the material and perceptual qualities of temporary events. The term is not limited to performance design because these principles and processes have become of interest and relevance to a variety of creative practitioners. In performance, scenography is no longer solely linked to designers, as a range of directors, choreographers, dramaturgs, writers and performance artists have integrated aspects of performance design in their practice. In parallel, a variety of other creative fields (such as the visual arts, architecture, fashion, media arts, curation and exhibition design) are increasingly including performance and performative events within their domains. This has resulted in their more or less explicit engagement with scenography. As such, scenography is a framework that is expanding in its application.

Whether applied in or out of the context of performance, the principles of a scenographic framework of practice remain the same; only its processes are likely to vary as they are adapted to the particulars of a given project. This book aims at clarifying these principles and sketching out these practical procedures loosely enough so as to be applicable in a range of contexts where temporary and performative events are concerned. As such, the practical insights and processes presented throughout the book do not constitute a particular methodology nor do they elaborate a complete description of the scenographic framework. Rather, the material contained in this book offers a series of actions found in performance design. These are articulated so as to be uniquely tailored to both your own interests and the particulars of a given creative process.

Accordingly, the book contains chapters describing the general purposes and uses of particular actions, interspersed by shorter texts written by contemporary practitioners who provide detailed tips and tasks based on their own practice. All of these practical strategies are stepping-stones to elaborate your own creative practice. Indeed, the book is aimed at creative practitioners who have an interest in, yet little or no practical experience of, scenography.

THE THREE PILLARS OF SCENOGRAPHY

Before we move on to discussing the practical tools and processes at play in a scenographic framework, some clarification of the principles that inform this framework is required.

One of the key principles in scenography is the live body. We design artefacts, environments and situations to be used, inhabited and observed by bodies. As such, the process of designing has to incorporate this bodily dimension, and for this to happen, a range of bodies (including ours) are mobilized. We might call this an *embodied* process, as we seek to hinge every step of the process on imagined and actual bodies. Importantly, here the body is not conceived according to a mundane, abstract or ideal standard. Quite the contrary, we approach bodies as diverse, dynamic, unique, creative and surprising organisms.

OPPOSITE: *Greek Precarious Body* by Olga Ntenta.

Whether they are performers or audiences or both at the same time, the bodies we work with are on a journey of discovery and transformation. We must, therefore, make as little assumption as possible about the body, including our own.

In effect, the preponderance of the body's experience in scenography is also part of a collaborative or *dialogic* principle that is also core to the scenographic framework. We engage in imaginary and actual collaborations, or dialogues, with bodies as well as spaces, texts, artefacts, materials and phenomena. More specifically, when we draw a body or model a space, these artefacts (drawing and model) are not finite but platforms that orchestrate a discussion between imagination (speculation) and realization (operation). Such artefacts project something imagined over something actual and, in doing so, generate all sorts of questions regarding both the imagined and the actual elements at play. The creative process then is driven by dialogues between speculative and operative modes of development. These dialogues tend to be more speculative at the start of the process and a lot more operative as we move towards completion. But in all cases they are conducted through actual materials that facilitate imaginative leaps.

There lies a third key principle in scenography, which is transformation. During the creative process, we transform or translate texts into situations, scale models into built environments, bodies into characters, sounds into images, materials into artefacts and so on. There is an overarching *transformative* principle inherent to a creative process developed under a scenographic framework. It includes, in particular, the layering or scaffolding of something new and temporary over something that already exists. But we can also see the transformative principle at work in the very outcomes of this process. Indeed, transformation is intrinsic to the time-based nature of scenographic work. The time factor implies that something must appear, evolve and disappear in the eyes of our audiences. Thus transformation is structural to the creative processes and outcomes of the scenographic viewpoint, which seeks to articulate 'a world where nothing is fixed and anything can happen' (Bogart and Landau 2005: 202).

PROFESSIONAL INSIGHT

DRAMATURGING
Henny Dörr

Henny Dörr is Course Leader of the Master in Fine Art and Design: Scenography at HKU University of the Arts, Utrecht, in the Netherlands. Since 1989, she has taught dramaturgy to scenographers. She is a founder and member of the interdisciplinary collective of artists Skilled/Unskilled, exploring artistic practice through performative research since 2013.

'What am I writing in space?' This is a vital question for a spatial practice that has to relate itself to narrative, meaning, semiotics and concepts. The risk: an over-emphasis on analysis, rationality, meaning and readability, leading to symbolism and intellectualism, and questions such as: Why is it this? Why did he/she do that? In which case, scenography becomes something to be motivated on a conceptual level: an art of the *head*.

But then, aside from the 'why', one can deal with 'what' and 'how': What do you want to make? What makes you stand out? What is your art about? What inspires you? What do you want to tell? What do you want to express? These are questions of the heart. What makes your (he)art tick? The answers might be seen as important for audiences, critiques, etc., but may be even more so as they are important to collaborate with other artists. The way these artists work influences the work itself and hence also your specific artistic contribution, and vice versa: what and how you contribute as an artist influences the way you work together. So, of equal importance are questions concerning this process of (co-)creation: How do I work best? How do I want to work? How does this group work? How do I influence this process? These 'how' questions necessarily translate into practical questions such as: When will I attend working sessions? How often? In what kind of environment do I want to work? What does my studio look like? Where is my studio? But also: What kind of materials do I want to work with? What kind of techniques? What do I need around me? Gradually, scenography comes back into the realm of the *hand*.

This leads to new thoughts and new ways of approaching the design process. As we tend to do things the way we are used to do things, there is much challenge and gain in engaging in a process of deconditioning. What if we assume the position of *not knowing*. Not knowing what to do, how to do it, what we want the result to be and so on. Can we then, through practice, find out what the true nature of our creative process is, and can we re-design it? Can we re-configure ourselves, in order to prevent us from working from assumptions, from answers we already have and from a design process that only produces variations on the same theme? Can we find a way to acknowledge that there are more ways of looking at something?

The act of observing is most important. This is not about one way of looking at things. Maybe the eye, for the designer, is what the body is for the dancer. And it might be that the eye and the mind become lazy, or economic. So it should be kept alert, to prevent it from starting to see what you are used to seeing.

Train the savage eye Look for the unfamiliar. This is a very important view, at the same time almost impossible, since we seem to understand the world on the basis of duality. We can understand the unfamiliar as that which is not familiar. Hence it is always set against the familiar through associations, interpretations, stories, aesthetics that you know. Something unusual reminds you of something familiar, yet in *looking for* that familiarity, you become aware of that which is unfamiliar. You might try to stop giving meaning to it, and just note and observe.

Try the objective eye This is a helpful way to obtain another reality than the one you make in your head: look at reality as a series of facts. Now, of course, the interesting part is that it opens up questions about what facts are, how many sorts of facts exist and where they stop to be facts. You will get a series of different lives of the world as objects: historical, biographical, material and social, and can even describe the senses or emotions as facts.

'Look for the unfamiliar.'

Feed the tactile eye Try and focus on one layer of reality, e.g. look in everything for sensations: tactility, temperature, mass, form, weight, anything that evokes a physical reaction. Do not forget that visuality is often key to what we are dealing with, so the question is not about what something feels like as such, but what something looks like that evokes a certain sensation.

You can elaborate other ways of looking by yourself. They give you the opportunity to look at things as if you see them for the first time, and open possibilities for designing a world. These tips may seem extremely obvious. But as soon as something enters the realm of the obvious, we risk not paying attention to it and we close our eyes to many discoveries and hidden worlds.

1
DRAWING

Drawing has a range of applications in scenography. We draw in response to a text, an image, a score or a concept. We draw observations of bodies, spaces and things around us. We draw imaginative ideas and events that might unfold. We draw the plans for the construction of something. So whenever we draw, the drawing is never an end in itself. Rather, the drawing in scenography is always in relation to something else that is actual or may be actualized/realized. In this sense, drawings mediate imagination and reality. They are meant to be *peered through* to assist the viewer in imagining an environment or artefact in concrete terms. They function as windows rather than as images. Yet drawings have limitations, as they can only ever loosely emulate the spatial and temporal parameters of scenographic work. Time and space can be hinted at in drawing but their design can only be finalized away from drawing, in actual terms.

Yet the need for our drawings to effectively become something real and tangible can create a sort of pressure on how we approach drawing: it can easily become an activity where we only draw that which can be realized. As such, drawing can be a rather mechanical practice. However, before drawing becomes instrumental in the passage to realization, its use as a creative practice, responding to a stimulus of a sort, is potentially crucial to creative developments. Indeed, it is within the imaginatively speculative dimension of a drawing that our ideas can be evolved to discover new forms.

OPPOSITE: *Miss Fortune* by Ana Maio.

A rough sketch, rapidly made on the page of a sketchbook or a napkin, may be rather incomprehensible to most, but to us it will have a significance of which we may be more or less aware. This is the beginning of a transformative dialogue with both a stimulus of sorts and our own imagination, which will lead us to unexpected outcomes.

Since drawings are bridges to projecting our imagination in potential or speculative environments, any drawing made without a concern for how it will translate in a realized form will trigger critical uncertainty regarding what it might be in reality. In other words, this kind of drawing will be either impossible to understand as a real structure or will suggest a variety of possible realized outcomes. This uncertainty is critical because it opens up the doors to creative exploration and development. And although technical drawing is far more instrumental, even so certain issues of realization might emerge and, yet again, these are problems to be solved creatively and thus provide opportunities to develop the work further.

Advocating the productive difficulty of translating an image into a three-dimensional and experiential environment is not only a matter of allowing creative developments. The challenge of shifting an impossible image into a possible event can be considered a key aspect of scenographic practice since, in theatre, this problem can be found within a wide spectrum of textual sources, ranging from divine apparitions in Ancient Greek plays to the ghostly ones of Shakespeare's. Unsurprisingly then, more recent playwrights have raised the stakes even further. Consider, for instance, the following stage direction written by the late Sarah Kane in *Cleansed* (1998): 'the rats carry Carl's feet away'. Though we can easily draw up a couple of rats running away with human feet in their mouth, if we also consider the realization of that image many problems emerge: How will Carl's feet be actually separated from his body? What will be the rats? How will they pick up Carl's feet? And so on.

These problems are not solely practical because whatever solution is found to translate this image will affect its impact and meaning. For example, we may want to consider designing puppets to represent the rats, but this could turn out to have a humorous effect that may not be appropriate. Thus, to approach this problem in the first instance, it would be best to not focus on a solution but rather engage in a dialogue with the uncertainty of the image. This also allows us to avoid the recycled clichés that often come with quickly conceived designs. It would not be surprising if the puppet solution to Kane's rats is one that hundreds of designers have considered. Indeed, images that easily come to our mind tend to be images we have been exposed to in our life. Because these are already lingering in our imagination with a great level of pre-existing details, they are easy to retrieve. As we are exposed and thus inhabited by so much imagery, it is difficult to resist recycling. A conscious effort in the way we engage in the creative process is required to minimize the influence of these ready-made images. And this effort must be concerned with not being too precise too quickly, and by allowing improvisation and experimentation at the core of the process.

One way of ensuring improvisation lies in considering our drawings in dynamic and kinetic terms, albeit in motion. From a scenographic standpoint, imagery is not static, not fixed, but always in movement. Historically, the tight relation between painting, architecture and theatre meant that static imagery was an expected component of the stage (e.g. flat, painted scenery). Yet, alongside that same history, multiple technical structures were invented to move this fixed imagery (e.g. flying systems). At the end of the nineteenth century, theatre practitioners like Edward Gordon Craig and Adolphe Appia decided to rid the stage from static painted scenery, instead focusing on the movement on stage. To do so, they both first used drawing to explore potentially new dynamics of space and light. However, prior to Craig and Appia, drawing was used to depict accurately the design to be. Craig and Appia, on the other hand, used drawing to grasp the action of a moment, to apprehend the potential of new dynamic phenomena on stage. Instead of perfectly defined shapes and surfaces, their drawings are concerned with volumes and movements of the intersection of the body, light and space. Rather than attempting to fix vision in a perspectival space, their drawings present us with how the human body may perceive this volumetric motion: movement being a shape in flux over time and space, the perception of depth and movement is more random and incomplete than the perception of stationary objects. In many ways, Craig and Appia's use of drawing is quite paradoxical, as they sought to inscribe three-dimensional and moving phenomena on flat and static paper. Yet this paradox is very productive, as it raises the creative potential of speculation over definition.

Throughout a creative project, from conception to completion, drawing can be utilized in this way to advance the design. It is likely, however, that drawing has a more important speculative role to play at the start of a project, with less and less allowance for the unknown being granted as the project evolves. In this chapter, we shall look at the practicalities of moving from the unknown to the known through various types of drawings needed during a project.

MOMENT DRAWING

A moment drawing is a drawing that seeks to grasp a scene or a particular instance in an event. Such drawing captures a movement of sorts. This may be based on an imagined moment, or one that is textually described, or one

IMPROVISATION AND TRANSFORMATION EXERCISE

Here is a quick practical exercise that will take you through a step-by-step journey of improvisation and transformation by drawing, providing you with simple rules to explore how something we know can be drawn to unpredictably become something else:

Step 1: to start with, you must select a stimulus that can be a text or an image (created by yourself or by someone else).
Step 2: on a sheet of paper, draw a table with five columns and name each column as follows: Vision, Touch, Smell, Taste, Sound.
Step 3: in each column, note down the specific sensory qualities expressed by the selected text or image (e.g. shiny in Vision, soft in Touch, burnt in Smell, sweet in Taste and noisy in Sound). You may add more qualities in some columns if needed.
Step 4: taking the selected text/image out of your sight, take a blank sheet of paper and draw a unique chair based on, and expressing, these specific sensory qualities. The challenge is to incorporate them all into an artefact that retains the function of hosting and resting one human body. The drawing must be detailed enough to express or suggest these qualities. Collage may be used. Careful attention must be paid to selecting the tools to be used for drawing. Watercolour, charcoal, ball pen, acrylic paint, markers, etc., have each inherent qualities that should be taken into account with respect to the specific sensory qualities required for your chair. The size and position of the drawing must be considered as if the sheet of paper was a space or a stage (though you do not need to emulate three-dimensionality in your drawing). The resulting chair should be most unusual, probably impossible and may not even look like a chair at all!
Step 5: on a new sheet of paper of the same size, and using the same drawing tools, morph the chair into a human body. The guiding framework here is the chair: all elements/aspects of the chair must mutate to form a body, which will have, as a result, all the specific sensory qualities identified before. This body should be as unrealistic as the chair before, thus it should be an impossible body of sorts.
Step 6: take the drawing of the chair out of your sight; on a new sheet of paper of any size, draw the cells of a storyboard. Now consider how the body you have drawn might move: what particular movement can this body do? Draw these movement variations sequentially in your storyboard. The result is likely to be a series of cells with rather abstract sketches that can now be observed as environmental elements and spatial structures.

that is actually observed. In any event, sketching an action is paradoxical: how does that which is in motion become visualized in a still image? We can choose to render the beginning of the action, its climax or its ending. But once a fragment of the action has been isolated, it is possible to see it as suggestive of another kind of action. Moment drawing is thus a slippery and speculative, rather definitive form. Nurturing this slipperiness can help us initiate design ideas. This has nothing to do with drawing skills but with the rules we employ in the way we draw the moment. For instance, in the case of a play text, we may select a handful of key moments/actions described in the text, and choose to draw only the outlines of the bodies and their environment, or only the bodies engaged in these moments without drawing their environment.

In moment drawings, we are not yet dealing with a complete aesthetic but with giving forms to particular actions. In doing so, some aesthetic features will emerge. Before developing these features further, it is worth improvising further with the already established features. In this case, we are looking for variations: how many other ways can there be to use these same features to present this particular action? Like for performers, improvisation for designers requires establishing certain rules – a framework. A drawing offers a framework in this respect: improvising with a drawing is done

Moment drawing by Samuel Beal sketching the outlines of a scene from Arthur Miller's *The Crucible* (1953). Note how the use of line drawing allows focusing on the action of bodies in space whilst suggesting the beginning of a spatial form occupying the floor and the background.

through new iterations and ways of re-assembling the same elements from the initial drawing.

Even though a moment drawing is somehow intuitive, it is also precisely conditioned by specific parameters. If we are looking to explore how an action might be staged, we can create additional rules to the improvisational approach to drawing. For instance, we might be interested in exploring an action from a variety of viewpoints or perspectives. Let's take a generic example: let's say that we want to improvise in drawing with the action of bare human feet walking in sand. Since this is an action we can easily see in everyday life, observation is a good starting point to drawing. We can observe both our own and someone else's feet walking in sand. This will generate more perspectives on the same action: observing our own feet will necessarily be done from above, thus offering an aerial view of the action; observing someone else's feet, on the other hand, can be done through a variety of viewpoints (any one of the possible positions all around the feet). Therefore, we would have at least two formal approaches to this moment drawing:

Character rendering by Khadija Raza depicting the protagonist of Georg Kaiser's *From Morning to Midnight* (1912). Although this drawing is suggestive of a costume, its purpose is rather to communicate a character. Note how the body's gesture represents a dynamic and active presence to which certain feelings can be associated. The expressive quality of the character is further enhanced by additional and colourful lines, seemingly radiating from its gesture. Also note the inclusion of texts that are key lines spoken by, and encapsulating, the character.

Speculative drawings by Sofia Esquivel exploring possible variations on the inclusion of bodies inside model boxes. Note how this idea is tried in relation to various body parts, as well as to one or more bodies, and to varying sizes of boxes.

- Starting from a square that would be the surface of the sand floor seen from above, we would draw the impact of feet on sand, the reliefs or sand dunes emerging around and above the feet, resulting in a type of topographic image or map. As this map is effectively the result of traces of feet in the sand, it then becomes possible to imagine how other actions of the feet in sand could create different maps. What kind of map emerges from my feet running or jumping on sand?

- Starting from a horizontal line that would be the surface of the sand floor, we would alter that line as different parts of the foot push into the sand, resulting in a series of shifting horizon lines or landscapes. In this case the softness of the ground becomes emphasized and, again, the horizon lines will vary according to the type of movement done by the feet in the sand.

Improvisation here can be further refined by selecting one specific action: we could decide to only approach this task in relation to a body jumping on

sand, still through the two perspectives mentioned above. This further defining of the framework does not stop improvisation, for we still have a range of phases of the jump to try out: Do we draw the feet lifting off the sand? Do we draw the first contact of the feet with the sand as they land? Do we draw the aftermath, once the jump has been completed? In the latter case, it is possible that the feet will be mostly covered by the sand that was pushed upwards by the landing and then fell back down over the feet. As such, this particular phase might, in drawing, be more reminiscent of a body buried under sand or emerging from the sand, rather than one that has jumped on the sand. This is where the speculative mode has allowed moving from a trivial/known action (walking on sand) to a different and less predictable situation (a body poking out of sand).

In turn, this newly discovered action can be further explored through drawing variations of the action. Observation may not be helpful in this case given the rarity and impracticality of human bodies emerging from sand. So the speculation here would need to rely on the actions of other organisms that do inhabit and emerge out of sand. We could draw a human body poking out of sand in the way of a sand crab (one limb at a time) or in the way of a razor

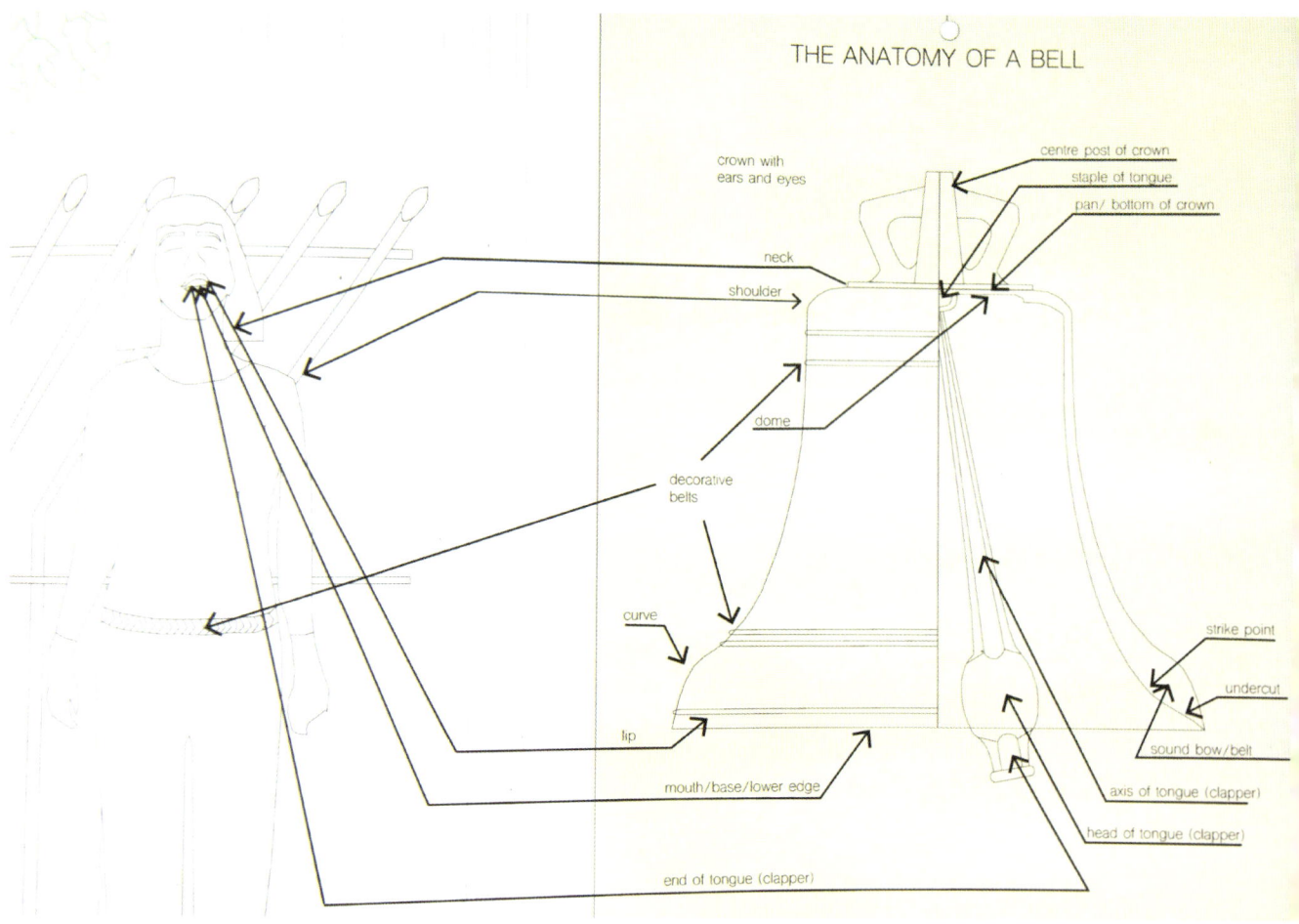

clam (all at once). As a result, we are now moving into even more impossible, yet new, ways of inhabiting and being in space.

The productive ambiguity of capturing movement on paper is enriched when we collide the moving presence of the human body with that of animals, objects, materials and so on. It allows us to refresh the human form and behaviour. To reconsider the movement of the body on a par with the motion of other elements (and vice versa), it may be helpful to guide ourselves by first establishing precise parallels between these two otherwise separate entities (and ways of moving). For instance, we can break down the different parts of an object and relate them to the different parts of a body: these relations may be about similarity in form or in motion or in function.

ABOVE: Speculative drawing by Lauren Tata. This is a schematic speculation regarding possible parallels that can be made between the various parts of an object (a bell) and those of a body. The drawing is suggestive of a potential of hybridization or fusion of the two entities.

OPPOSITE: Speculative drawing by Lauren Tata. Here the visual association of a bell and a body into one singular structure is now visualized with the suggestion of a wearable bell-like outfit.

DRAWING SPACE

Drawing can also facilitate shifting the development of the design into three-dimensional considerations. When we draw a space, we are inherently trying to push a sheet of paper (or any other surface we may use) to exude three-dimensionality. There is a paradox here that can be daunting. But there are many ways by which we can approach the paper sheet as if it was a window, an interface to peer through and envision an actual space. This is about training our eyes to not see the sheet of paper as a two-dimensional surface but rather as a sort of three-dimensional haze that can be carved by a pencil. Such training can be done with the basic starting point of drawing cubes with one or more open sides. These provide us with visual guidelines of both the frame and the axial depth within that frame. At the same time, such open cubes offer interesting challenges, as it is likely that any image we may want to include within the cube will need to be adjusted to it and may appear quite different from what it was previously.

After drawing quite a lot of these open cubes, they become monotonous canvases teasing us to challenge and complicate them. This then brings us to the scenographic layering of spatial environments. Layering can be considered on the horizontal and vertical planes of the cube: for instance, breaking down the floor into multiple areas (traditionally a foreground, a midground and a background) and breaking down the volume of space into multiple new stages of various heights (called levels in scenic design). Layering allows us to create multiple spaces out of one, and only one, environment. And this can have the effect of exploding the base environment (the cube) or it can be still neatly contained within it. Generally, layering disrupts the perception of the cube whenever certain layers exceed the frame of the cube and, therefore, seem to extend well beyond it. Even then, an awareness of the cube we are working in is helpful since it is a now invisible (or near invisible) part of the work.

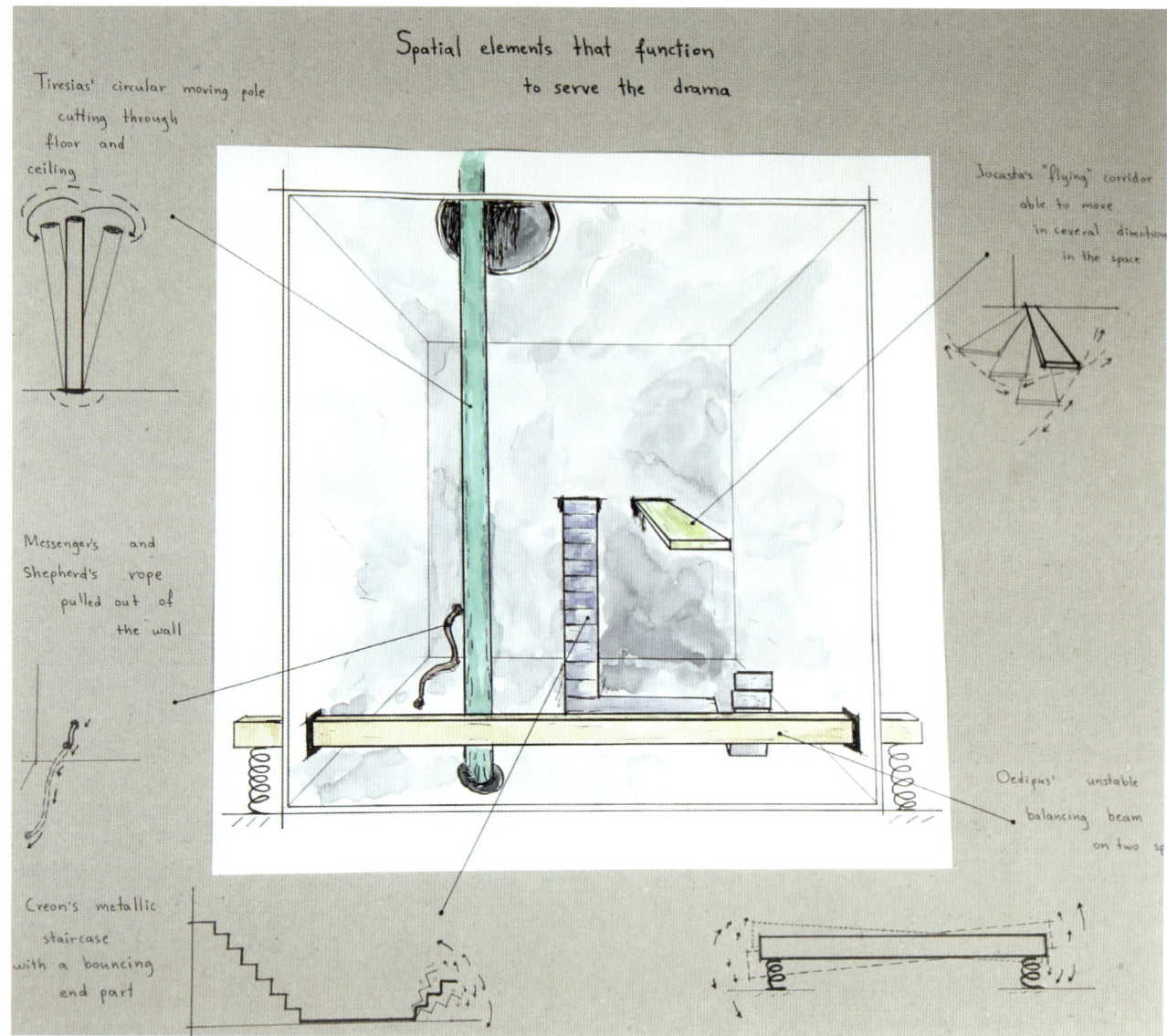

Speculative drawing by Olga Ntenta. Note how the cube provides a frame for three-dimensional speculation as it pushes us to engage with volume and depth.

Other features of the cube may become monotonous and, as a result, be creatively modified. For instance, the symmetry of the cube's outlines may be used as coordinates for an exploration of scenic symmetry or to be disrupted by asymmetry. Similarly, the height and depth it suggests may be emphasized, reduced or even erased. So, our open cubes are only there to provide the three-dimensional frame we must stay aware of, whether it has relevance to our design endeavour or whether we want to break away.

Whereas previous drawings were based on perceptual and embodied viewpoints (the actual viewpoint of bodies, spectating or performing), the open cubes allow us to expand viewpoints to incorporate an omnipresent point of view, close to the rather divine perspective of the aerial viewpoint or bird's-eye view. As we draw elements into the cubes, we can more easily consider their positions and distances to one another via a more easily imagined bird's-eye view. The aerial viewpoint is somewhat the least rational perspective (unless, of course, we are aiming to have our audience looking down on the work) and thus it is often utilized in the form of maps or ground plans, the technical function of which is to locate and position the design precisely. However, the aerial or bird's-eye view that determines mapping also provides a creative platform for developing the design. In this case, the aerial viewpoint is taken into account well before the physical set up has been defined. Though this viewpoint is rarely experienced by audiences, for the designer it is one more perspective through which design ideas can be initiated, transformed and developed. Going back to the example of the action of stepping into sand, seen from an aerial viewpoint, the softness of the ground would no longer be emphasized. Instead, we may find a flatter and more geometric imagery emerging. And rather than enabling the perception of a body emerging out of the sand, this aerial imagery may point towards a body as a calligraphic tool, since its presence is revealed by the traces, lines and shapes (revealed aerially) the body leaves in the sand. Accordingly, we may start speculating about more unusual bodily movements and the more unusual marks these would make in the sand.

OPERATIVE DRAWING

At some point in the creative process, drawing must become more entangled with actual and determinant factors, such as performing bodies that are starting to be arranged in particular ways (directed or choreographed). In the context of rehearsals, capturing performers in space via an aerial view can be essential to start defining the exact positions and actions of the design ideas we are developing for these bodies. In addition to pinpointing the locations of performers on the ground, we can also highlight the axis of performers moving from one location to another. As we try to map the performer's travelling axis from above, we can see specific shapes emerging; these may be angular/harsh or curved/soft, or actual circles or triangles may even become apparent. In some sense, these provide us with a more global understanding of the structured spatialization of the performers (also known as the blocking). Just as importantly, we can use these shapes created by bodies within the design elements.

We may conceive of the scenography as a visual structure that merges with the blocking or contrast with it. In the first case, we would draw these forms into the design. In the second case, we would elaborate opposite forms and qualities. In both cases, there are many ways by which the scenography can emphasize or contrast with the shapes generated by performers. Emphasis and contrast become frameworks but both can be achieved more or less conspicuously. Thus much of the speculative drawing then becomes targeted towards the consideration of subtle, moderate and bold emphasis or contrast. There is also the possibility of the scenography both emphasizing and contrasting at the same time. The more variations on this idea, the more surprises may come up. However, exploring these variations is likely to require a shift of viewpoint, back to a frontal perspective. And in this shift, again, lies all sorts of problems and questions: an idea exacted in an aerial view would need to be further elaborated in a frontal view, since there are many surfaces and forms that are essential to render frontally but which are invisible aerially.

Less speculative in kind, this type of drawing is operative because it starts the process of settling fixed parameters that may pre-exist the design or may, in fact, be core elements of the design. Operative drawing incorporates a more precise physical framework that is partly technical. It functions as a trigger to three-dimensional work inasmuch as it includes visual elements to be physically explored. The level of actual experimentation such

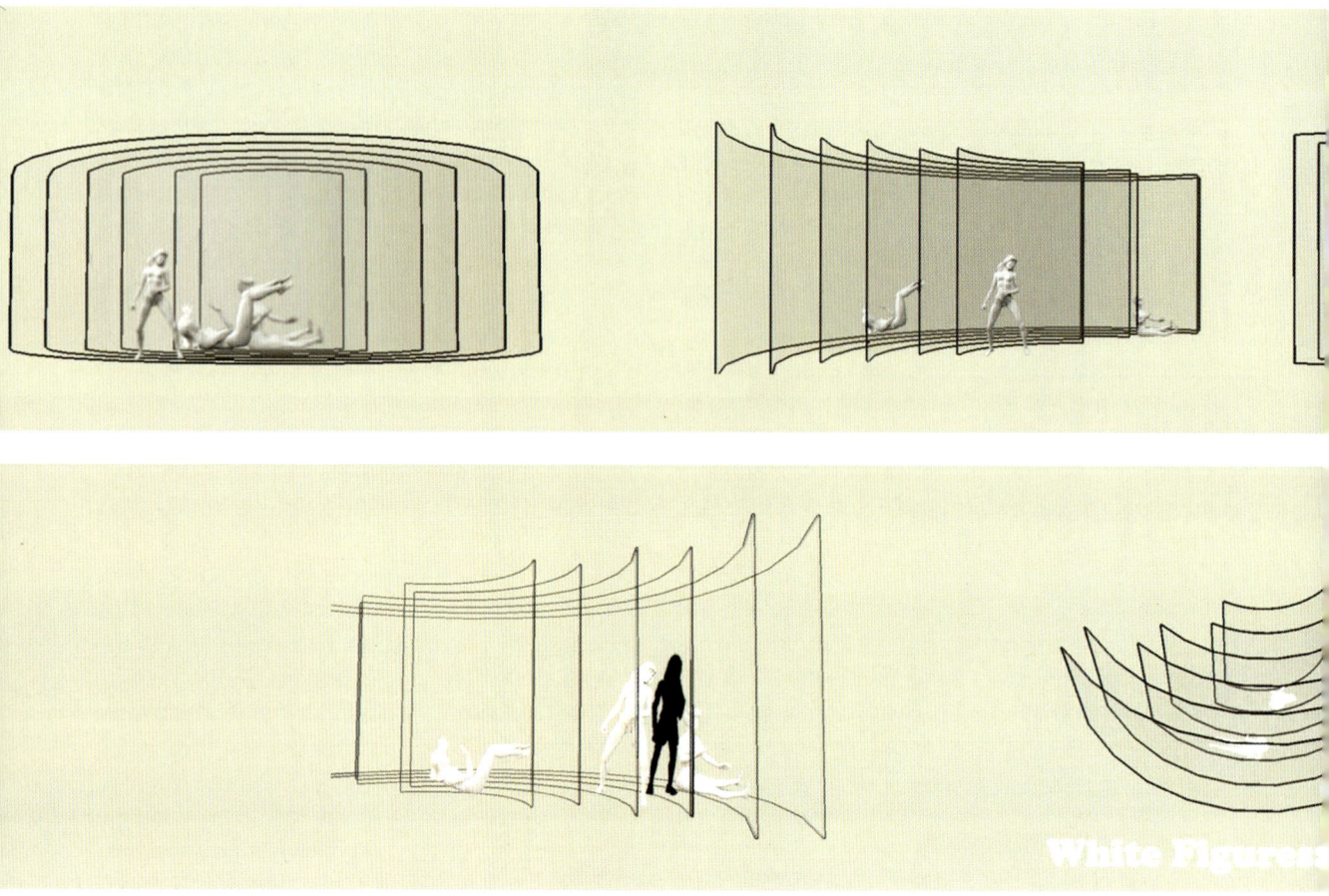

Operative drawings by Rea Olympiou depicting multiple viewpoints on a spatial structure with spectating and performing bodies. The aerial viewpoint is used to clarify the form of the structure, whilst the other viewpoints denote the various angles from which the structure can be seen (indeed this is a site-specific design where audiences can freely circulate all around, as well as through, the structure).

drawing can offer varies, depending on the type of operation it supports. There are two main types of operative drawings: those that present a particular structure in which visual effect is uncertain and will need to be prototyped, and those that render precise visual effects in which physical set up is uncertain and, again, will need to be prototyped. Either way, the operative drawing mediates the transition from imaginative speculation to material prototyping and physical realization. This is, therefore, a more controlled type of drawing that serves as a more direct engagement with what will become realized. Some precision is required to outline some of the elements that define the parameters of the framework (position of bodies, architectural or atmospheric features of the environment, required artefacts and so on). Whereas the speculative drawings in the previous section cannot be straightforwardly translated into three-dimensional experiments, the drawing approach here is precisely aimed at facilitating the transition to real scale with more or less improvisational potential still included within it.

However precise and certain, an operative drawing is still just a drawing and, as such, it cannot fully anticipate the work to be realized; further refining will be needed during the realization process. However, such drawing is not only able to

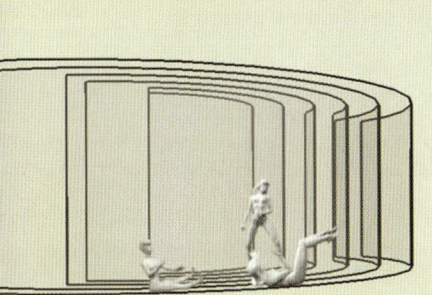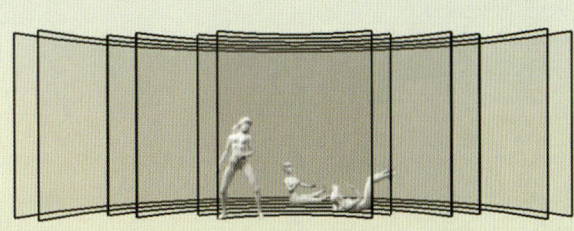
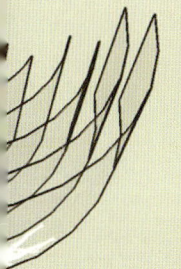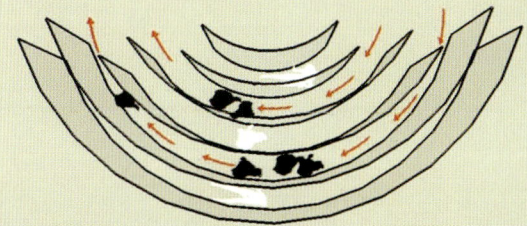

Dancers Black Figures: Audience **Arrows:** Audience Corridor

guide realization but, just as importantly, and before realization starts off, operative drawings are particularly useful tools for communication. Their degree of precision regarding settled elements of the design can help our collaborators. For instance, operative drawings allow us to discuss with constructors and makers the different options for realizing prototypes/mock-ups and eventually the final artefact. This is particularly important in terms of identifying modes of construction that may have an impact on the design, thus modifying it slightly. To this end, drawing the front view of the costume is insufficient and should be complemented by a view of the back. A side view may also be relevant if particular details are found on the sides or, in the case of a mask, if the three-dimensionality of the artefact cannot be properly ascertained from the frontal view.

Operative drawings are also useful images to present and discuss with performers and directors. These collaborators are evidently concerned with what will be materially integrated on stage since this will have a meaningful, as well as physical, impact on the actions to be staged. But different collaborators have different concerns and so our operative drawings often need to be edited for the purpose of a particular collaborator. An actor, for instance, will be concerned with how their costume relates to their character, as well as how they might move in that costume. Thus, for actors, it is recommended to produce separate drawings of each costume, otherwise called costume rendering. In this way, the actor sees the drawing as a fictional self-portrait that is a portrait of their character. Such drawing should present the body and costumes in a movement that is relatable to that character. And to enhance the actor's identification with the drawing, it is helpful to bring certain features of the actor's body into the drawing: the body shape, height and proportions can be as useful as simply drawing the actor's face.

OPPOSITE: Costume rendering by Reuben Speed depicting the ensemble of all the costumes designed for Georg Kaiser's *From Morning to Midnight* (1912). Note how the characters are expressed through precise costumes and accessories but also through gestures and facial features, as well as through grouping. Also note how the floor and background communicate an environment shared by this ensemble. Given the contrasts that split the two groups sharing that same environment, we can deduce what the conflicts of this drama might be.

BELOW: Costume rendering by Lia Waber depicting the ensemble of characters and costumes designed for Botho Strauss' *The Park* (1983). Note how the drawing is suggestive of an environment without an attempt at rendering a three-dimensional space. This environment is clearly shared by all the characters, yet we can see from the costumes and the spacing between them that they are grouped in pairs.

ABOVE: Costume rendering by Magdalena Iwanska presenting the costume and character of Death in Botho Strauss' *The Park* (1983). Note how the costume is communicated with clear and simple lines, precise motifs and colours, and against a background that is suggestive of a spatial design. Also note how the character is represented by way of a dynamic position, seemingly in the midst of moving or turning around, thereby causing slight distortions and movement to the fabrics.

DRAWING 25

Rendering of the progression of a character's costumes by Reuben Speed. Note that this character is the protagonist of Ibsen's *A Doll's House* (1879); as such her costumes are visually prevailing and thus central to communicating the evolution of the plot. PATRICK BALDWIN

However, a director's concern with costumes is more likely to be related to the visual associations between costumes and the coherence of all the costumes in the space. Thus, in this case, it is worth producing a drawing that includes all the costumes at once (as an ensemble) with spatial references related to the environments they will inhabit: this includes backgrounds as well as floors, since the costumes will be seen against these surfaces.

Grouping costume renderings within one image can also help us refine the designs: we can more easily see and adjust differences in colours, textures and sizes to enhance or reduce contrasts. In a similar fashion, when a performer is expected to be wearing different costumes at different times, it is worth grouping the various costumes of the said character in the order they will occur. This will expose the overarching design, as well as, again, the differences that may need to be enhanced or reduced.

Finally, operative drawings are likely to be accompanied by notes and sample materials so as to hint even more strongly towards their actual realization. But however precise the drawings, notes and samples may be, the design is not completed yet – it will be refined up to completion through the next phases of the process with storyboarding, modelling, prototyping and realizing.

STORYBOARDING

So far, our approach to drawing has been concerned with creative speculation and rendering moments, bodies and spaces. There is one more scenographic dimension that can be partially designed through drawing: time. Typically, storyboards are a form of drawing that is suggestive of the different stages through which an image or situation might evolve. Try to capture

Storyboard by Meera Osborne depicting, from observation, the breakdown of a body's movements. By unpicking every gesture in a linear fashion, it is possible to decipher patterns and rhythmic structures.

in drawing the changing gestures of a body and you will immediately touch on the most basic form of storyboard.

For this reason, storyboards are highly relevant to time-based works such as performance and film. At the end of the nineteenth century, theatre director Constantin Stanislavski and film-maker Georges Méliès created storyboards to plan different kinds of timely progression: naturalistic (and theatrical) in Stanislavski's case; surrealistic (and filmic) in the case of Méliès. This alerts us to the fact that whether we are dealing with unrealistic/irrational or natural/logical timing, it is important to anticipate how timing will be executed.

Although the sense of time can be manipulated, the timely structure of theatre and film has a linear foundation. Thus, structurally, storyboards are sequential: they depict moments in a chronological and linear fashion, through a grid-like structure of cells or vignettes. However, storyboards for films can differ from those made for theatre. The outline of the cells or vignettes of film storyboards represent the frame of the camera. Thus each cell informs where the camera will be located, as well as the camera settings (as well as lenses and filters) that will be required to achieve that image. On the other hand, in storyboards for theatre, each cell is a viewpoint that pertains to the spectator. As such, a cell might show the entirety of the stage or just a segment as a way to suggest what we want the spectator to focus on. The outline of the cells in theatrical storyboards may also represent the proscenium arch or, in the absence of one, how the architecture/environment frames the performance or nothing in the case of outdoor/open-air events. In the case of a design for a proscenium arch theatre that creatively includes the proscenium arch (probably modified in some way), the proscenium arch would be drawn and included within the content of the cell.

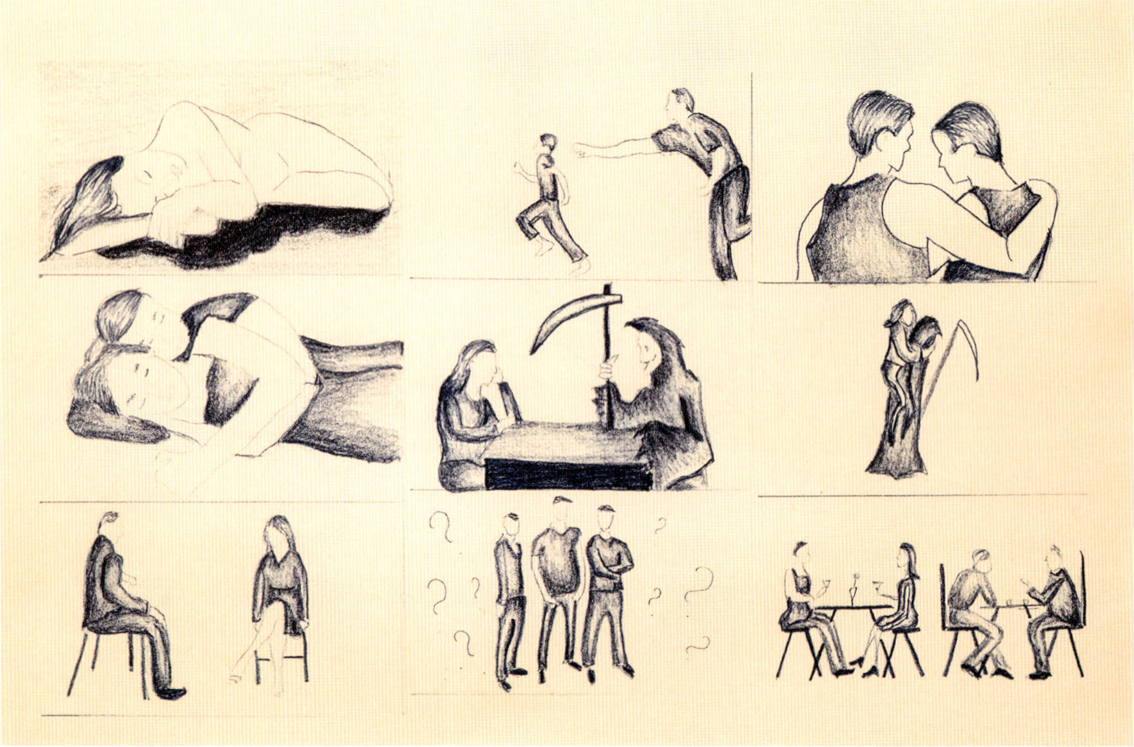

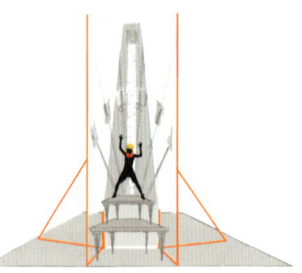
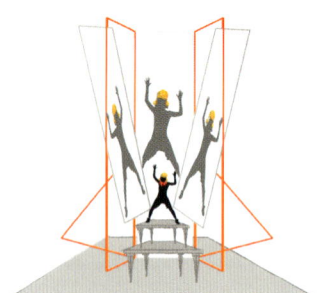

ABOVE: Speculative storyboard by Magdalena Iwanska depicting key moments in Botho Strauss' *The Park* (1983). Note that the storyboard focuses on bodies in physical actions and situations, only including additional elements that are absolutely necessary to these situations (such as tables and chairs).

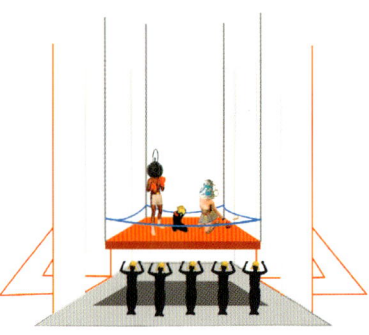

Though the storyboard offers some degree of precision in some aspects (audience perspective, framing and so on), its rendering of time and transformation is suggestive so as to be further defined later on in real space and time. Whilst it can, therefore, be a functional tool for anticipating and preparing the next phases of realization, it is also, as a result of its suggestiveness, pertinent to speculating for the purpose of design developments. Speculative storyboards are another form of drawing practice relevant to use as part of our initial response to a text, image or concept. In such storyboards, very little has been designed yet but we are starting to improvise with the backbones of what the design will need to concern itself with. Speculative storyboards also allow us a preview of the scope and number of transitions that will be required for the entire progression of the work.

As static visuals, drawn storyboards can never be absolutely precise about time. Operative storyboards can offer a more precise vision of the transformation of a design over a timeframe that remains somehow speculative.

Producing such a detailed storyboard will be of use to a range of collaborators: it will give performers and directors an understanding of the overall scheme of the world to be staged; it will enable other designers to further define their contribution to this world; it will be a useful document to discuss with technical collaborators in view of identifying the best ways to construct, manage and operate that world. Just as importantly, for ourselves, this kind of storyboard is an ideal stepping stone to further defining the three-dimensional and timely dimensions of our designs via modelling in scale.

BELOW: Operative storyboard by Dallas Wexler showing the progression of scenic design for Maurice Ravel's *L'Enfant et les Sortileges* (1925). Note how bodies are clearly positioned and located within this storyboard. The storyboard clarifies both how the set is changing, as well as how it is occupied and inhabited. However, the timeframes for these various scenes and their transitions remain speculative.

 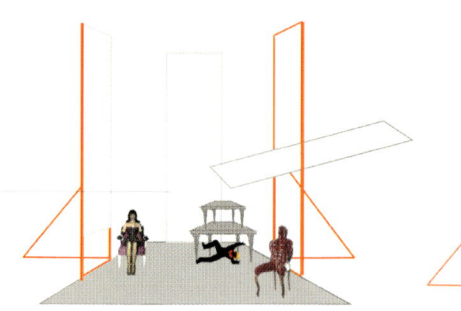 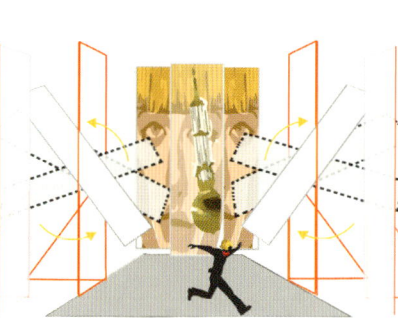

 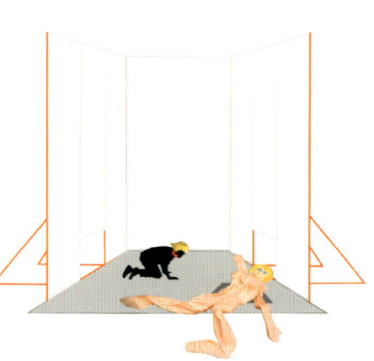 

PROFESSIONAL INSIGHT

LISTENING
Dan Scott

Dan Scott's work incorporates installation, performance, and participatory practice, and often investigates the politics and poetics of listening. He has carried out projects internationally, including recent projects: Liberation through Hearing, outside the Royal Academy in London; Yesterday at Harewood House in Yorkshire; Speak What You Find (with Magic Me) in London; the monthly event Athelstan Sound in Margate; and the Sonic Trails series at Tate Modern.

In my work, listening is used as a technique, like drawing or writing, and I employ all manner of modes, strategies and tactics in its application, derived from sound art, improvised music, communications theory and beyond. Such a focus on listening is not intended as a reductive exercise, listening is not used instead of seeing, smelling, tasting or touching. Rather, a listening approach offers a particular perspective that can be generative and inspiring to a designer.

Listening leads to different ways of sensing across modalities. Listening may lead to different ways of seeing (e.g. looking for what is heard over what is visually noticed) or to noticing the many overlaps between what is heard and what is felt as touch. Listening is also particular and partial, it is as much part of social class, gender, sexuality and constructed self, as well as the complex and partial identities of those who listen and who are listened to, as it is of any essential or physiologically determined aspect of self. Listening creates a space for reflexive awareness. Listening can mean a pause in discourse and it's in listening that you learn to think, reflect and allow the world to resonate, altering you in the process.

Listening creates spaces: a particular listening engaged by a particular individual or group (e.g. an audience) will create a particular type of space. In the case of a musical performance, it is the listening of the music lover – her eyes forward (or closed), her attention on the musicians and not the breath of the person sitting next to her – that affords the music its meaning, and its particular presence in that space. The space of a musical performance is as much as a space made by listening as it is space made by sound.

The following exercise draws attention to the existing soundscape of a given location, highlighting what potential already exists in that space for design and performance, and is an example of how to use listening to create scenographic space.

The exercise begins with a performance of composer Pauline Oliveros' Environmental Dialogue, a participatory text score that leads a group through a form of listening meditation, focusing on sounds inside and outside a given space. Oliveros has argued (Oliveros 2010: 74):

Two modes of listening exist, focal listening and global listening. Focal listening provides details through concentration on single sounds, whereas global listening provides context through concentration on the entire field of sound. When both modes are utilized and in balance with one another, the listener is in connection with all existence

Environmental Dialogues engages with both of those modes, and is one of many examples of her practice of 'deep listening'. The piece is most effective with two or more people, and is performed as follows (Oliveros 1971: 344):

Each person finds a place to be, either near to or distant from the others, either indoors or out-of-doors. Begin the meditation by observing your own breathing. As you become aware of sounds from the environment, gradually begin to reinforce the pitch of the sound source. Reinforce, either vocally, mentally or with an instrument. If you lose touch with the source, wait quietly for another. Reinforce means to strengthen or sustain. If the pitch of the sound source is out of your range, then reinforce it mentally.

Begin the piece with a short and focused introduction of silent listening. Begin by listening to the sounds of your body, as well as other's in the space (breathing, rustling, etc.), then attend to sounds at the boundaries of the space. Next, focus on the sounds outside the space, and finally to the most distant sounds you can hear. This listening meditation moves attention through the space: from bodies, to boundaries, to distant and sometimes even imagined sounds.

Once a range of sounds has been perceived, begin working through Oliveros' score. Find a sound and begin voicing it, gradually increasing in volume, placing the sounds in dialogue with other people's sounds, before drawing them back into silence.

After performing *Environmental Dialogues*, use the experience to inform the creation of a sound map. A sound map is a topographical representation of the sounds present in a space. Like any form of cartography, sound maps can be empirical in their methodology – sound maps exist for noise levels across cities, or to represent animal noises in particular ecosystems – or they can be highly subjective. For our purposes, the content and mode of the map is up to the designer. It could represent each sound source – a foot, a car, a fan – or it could represent the grain and density of sounds in the space, or the feelings, associations or memories these sounds engender in the listener. The process is open, but all the maps begin with placing the listener at the centre of the page. The creation of the sound-map offers a space for the particularity of the individual's listening to emerge – it's not intended as an objective act of classification.

Once the sound map is completed, consider it a score. The focus now shifts from representing what exists in the space, and in the bodies of those who listened, to using that map as a precursor for a new space. Here, as you re-interpret the maps as graphic scores, those initial listenings become resolutely active and generative. The form of re-interpretation can be dictated as per the needs of the design and the project: the content of the maps can be considered still in relation to sounds, or as movements, spatial structures, lighting phenomena, configuration of objects, and so on.

Listening can be viewed as a non-productive activity, and because of this, can be ignored in favour of noisier and more industrious acts of *making*. I have been developing these practices of listening in the spare moments of my working life where, all too often, the high-pace, time-short process of devising, making and performing does not allow for such expansive and speculative moments of reflection and creation. So much of production is *sounding* – talking, offering opinion, the bang and clatter of making – and doesn't afford space for a careful listening to occur. They require trust and time. I do not suggest these techniques are novel or revolutionary in themselves (some are common in devising workshop scenarios), rather that a more prolonged and 'deep' engagement with listening can become a radical way of working when used as the primary approach for design. As outlined above, such an approach can inform visual design, or movement, or narrative, as much as the aural. Moreover, it can shift the interpersonal relationships of those involved in a production from hierarchies of speaker to listener, and towards more open dialogical interactions and ways of working.

2
MODELLING

Typically, scale models support the transition from the two-dimensionality of drawings and sketches to three-dimensionality. To this end, models anticipate the real-scale realization of the design and seek to communicate it to others. Yet, at the same time, they bring forth certain conditions that couldn't be properly taken into account in drawing and that are likely to require altering the design: for instance, the spaces given to bodies within the design and the resulting viewpoints (or sightlines) become more precisely demarcated in a model. To this extent, scale models can enable a greater level of detail to be perceived, as well as the rapid alteration of general or detailed elements. Scale models are meant to be physically interacted with. Thus, although models can appear to be finite structures, they nonetheless offer possibilities for variation on a given design and thus can support further the creative process prior to completing the design.

SCALE

For these reasons, in theatre design, scale models tend to be used at two different stages of the process: first, as white card models during the phase of conception, and then as complete scale models for the purpose of realization and completion. Yet, at both stages, scale models remain partly unreliable, simply due to the fact that the scale prevents the visibility of certain details. Thus

OPPOSITE: *The Mirror Skin*, model figure by John Smith.

a design can never be fully completed via a scale model. Whichever kind of model we are using, we must always remain aware that a certain amount of detail is necessarily missing due to the scaled condition of the model. These missing details must be considered as we build the model because they may inform the way the model should be constructed and otherwise may become significant problems later on. In a model, it is often tempting, for example, to design singular and continuous surfaces that cover the entire floor or ceiling or backwall. However, in real scale, it is almost never possible to construct such scenic elements, simply because materials do not exist in such large dimensions. They come in pieces of smaller dimensions, which will, therefore, need to be connected to one another to create the overall effect. Yet that effect may no longer be as effective due to what has been added to the edges of the material pieces to connect them. Knowledge of the maximum dimensions in which materials can be obtained is, of course, important. On the other hand, we should not avoid large and continuous surfaces, as these are possible to emulate under certain conditions, depending on the materials and how the surfaces are used.

Patterns are another problem when it comes to details. Whether we create a pattern directly in scale or we scale down an existing pattern, scaled patterns will offer a wide range of gaps once transposed in real scale. Furthermore, what may appear as a dot on a scaled tapestry in a model, could be a range of things in real scale: a plain circle, a stain, a cherry, a flower and so on. This is why a final model should be accompanied by technical documentation and samples or prototypes that can clarify the problems posed by the details in the model.

Although in a model materials cannot be exactly the same as the real materials that will be used to realize the design, similarities must be sought after as much as possible: a textile artefact should be modelled with fabric, glass with plastic, metals with aluminium, wood with balsa wood and so on. Evidently, if a wooden floor is meant to be unrealistically painted over a linoleum floor, then the modelled version of that design will not use balsa wood but a plastic surface. With more natural materials, such as soil or sand, the scale-modelled equivalent will be brown pigments. Paper should be used for dry leaves and so on. In the model, we need the materials to help us understand the qualities of the actual materials to be used – not only the visual qualities (opacity/transparency, texture, reflectivity, mirroring, etc.), but also the physical qualities, such as scale, weight and motion. In this way the model can be an effective communication tool, as well as a creative tool to define the design further. It may, indeed, become a helpful artefact to a range of collaborators too.

Models are meant to help us envision real-scale environments – they are tools rather than artefacts. Though they can be technically approached in many different ways, they should not be comprised of unnecessary details that would make it difficult to imagine the design in real space. At the same time, the scale of models makes it impossible to be fully accurate, so we are looking to reduce the quantity and quality of these discrepancies to a minimum, while maximizing the quantity and quality of accuracy. Scale should help us read the models, not the opposite. So the choice of

OPPOSITE: Scale model by Vivianna Chiotini. The key materials at play in the design (garden and curved mirror walls) have been replicated as realistically as possible so that the design's visual phenomena can be perceived and understood. Note that lighting is also crucial in this case since its position and direction dictate whether the visual phenomena of reflection appear or not. PATRICK BALDWIN

Model in scale 1:25 by Alice Simonato. Note how the scenic design is made of really tall panels, that could easily dwarf the performers but they have been painted in such a way that their upper halves are a lot less visible than their bottom halves. The inclusion of scale figures further helps to consolidate the focus of attention to the ground.

scale for any model must be considered carefully. Not every scale is appropriate to any kind of design. The choice of scale must be made on the basis of the details we want to show and the size of the space/environment that needs to be represented by the model: for instance, scale 1:100 is useful for models representing large spaces and structures, whereas smaller spaces are best dealt with the scale 1:25. Furthermore, there is another criterion of selection to keep in mind here: the chosen scale must be practical enough for human hands to pick up and move components around without disturbing the model. Effectively, the clarity of any chosen scale relies on the presence of scale figures positioned within the model. Without these, the scale of any design cannot be properly understood and, as a result, the dimensions of the design cannot be fully evaluated.

White card model in scale 1:100 by I-Shun Lee. Note how the communication of the enormous space of Tate Modern's Turbine Hall here is supported by the inclusion of scale figures, as well as precise lighting.

WHITE CARD

The white card model, as its name suggests, is predominantly white and constructed out of simple and mobile materials, such as card. Only key design elements can be introduced in their actual colours and textures. The white card model thus presents an incomplete design that requires further manipulation and definition. Its material simplicity and whiteness are intended to provoke improvisation and experimentation. To this end, most components of the white model should be loosely attached in order to be rearranged. Like the open cubes discussed in Chapter 1, the white card model is likely to be an open cube or box of sorts, wherein the actual surfaces that make up the cube/box can be removed so as to be able to observe the model from a variety of angles.

While the box needs to be physically solid and robust, everything else inside of it must have enough material flexibility that it can be easily modified on the spot. Modelling materials that can be rapidly altered include: card, paper, foam, balsawood, as well as more recent kinds of so-called smart materials, such as polymorph, metal paper and shape memory cold-forming plastics. If there are internal features that are part of the overall physical (and immobile) framework, then these may be constructed in a more permanent fashion using mountboard and PVA glue (avoid other glues like super glue as this is too abrasive for the materials we are using, i.e. the glue will damage the materials). Glue should be avoided for everything else; instead pins should be used for temporarily connecting elements. Pins tend to be more adequate than masking tape or tack because they are stronger yet lighter. In addition, pins are unlikely to have an effect on the surfaces that are pinned, whilst tape and tack may be too adhesive or not adhesive enough, they may also add thickness or simply not hold surfaces together sufficiently. Lightweight elements of the model, on the other hand, may be best attached with bits of tack or masking tape. It is important that all elements of the model can be quickly removed and reattached. One practical challenge here relates to the stability of the model's content. Because we do not want the content to be permanently fixed, it is likely that many components will not stand in the model by themselves (especially while modifications are made), thus requiring temporary support. Such support may be a scaled down version of a traditional brace or French brace, or a small-scale equivalent to a weight.

The inherent flexibility of the white card model makes it an ideal artefact to pursue experimentation with the dynamics of space and time. Rather than defining an image further, the white card model allows focusing on the three-dimensional and temporal dimension of the image: the appearance, progression and disappearance of visual phenomena. Indeed, in the white card model, new and crucial questions can be asked with respect to the speculative intersection of body and space: entrances and exits, or how bodies appear and disappear.

Entrances and exits are not only a matter of doors and door frames, but of the very opening and closing of moments and of the event itself. In theatre, the opening and closing of a curtain is a traditional signal for the appearance and disappearance of the event. Though there are many alternatives to curtains nowadays, it is important to highlight the kinetic and, therefore, temporal dimension of the curtain. Indeed, curtains expose and conceal the stage by way of moving or drawing in and away. This is different from the flash appearance of a slide show or a film. The moving presence of curtains allows transitioning, back and forth, between the reality of the audience and that of the stage in a timely manner. This transitioning principle is crucial because it is inherent to the very temporal progression or evolution of images on stage. To this extent, the transition from one visual phenomenon to another must be designed, as it is part of these visual phenomena, if not a visual phenomenon in itself. Therefore, the more materially flexible the white model is, the more profitable

White card model, aerial view by Rita Torrao, presenting a snake-like structure in a site-specific location. Note how, unlike the rest of the model, the structure has been carefully modelled with materials of relevance to the design. In a site-specific context, the aerial viewpoint is often essential because it provides an overall view, which cannot be obtained from any other viewpoint. From this image, we can see that the tight space around the structure would prevent the visitor on the ground from ever perceiving the entirety of the structure.

White card model, elevation view by Rita Torrao. Here the view is from the ground but it is not the view of the visitor: note how a long wall has been removed in order to reveal another comprehensive overview of the design that would otherwise be blocked by that wall.

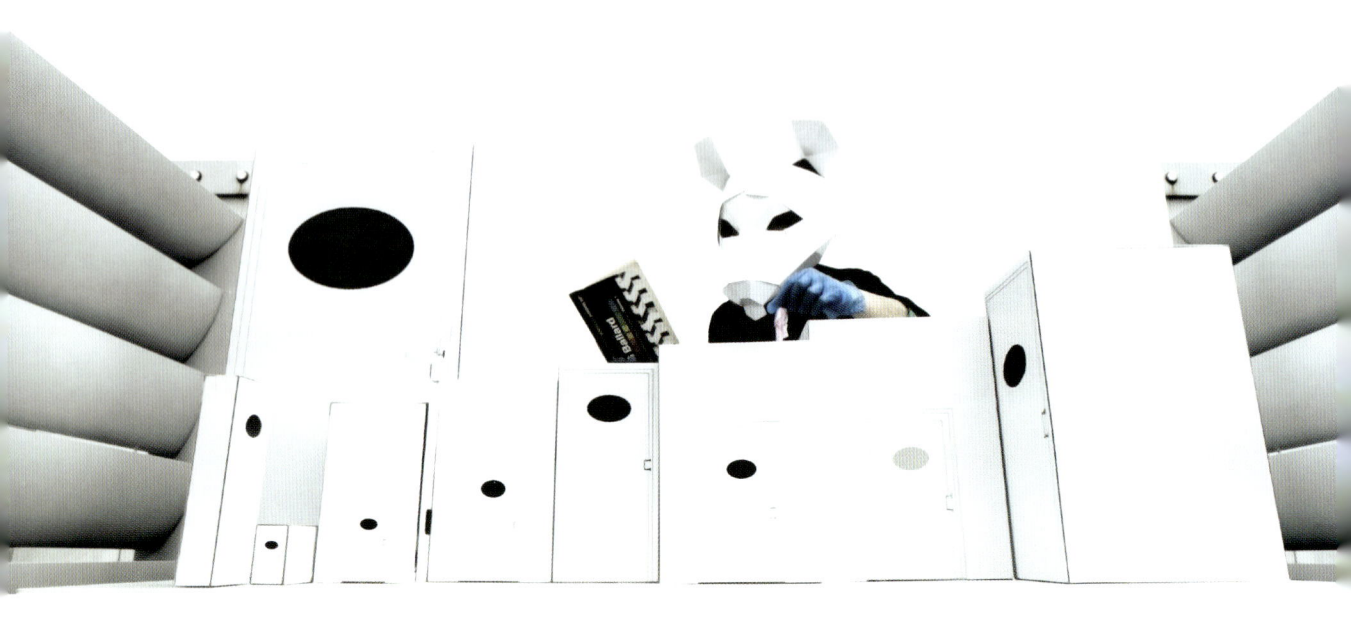

White card model by Sofia Esquivel. Entrances and exits are essential devices for the appearance and disappearance of the body. Here a multiplicity of modelled doors and door frames is used to explore variations on an excessive amount of entrances and exits.

Scale model by Alice Cousins. The multiplicity of props (boxes and papers) can be helpful in trying out different arrangements and refining the quantities accordingly. Also note how common props can also provide reference points for understanding the scale of a space. PATRICK BALDWIN

White card model by Marina Mattos. Quickly made wire figures are useful whenever the body is visualized to simply demonstrate the spatial locations it can inhabit. The scale figures included in this model are precisely there to signal the simultaneous use of two floors. Also note: to expose two floors that can otherwise only be seen separately, a wall shared by these two floors has been removed. This results in a section model, which allows us to perceive relations designed between the two floors, from the point of views of either floor. And, indeed, the design here is located within an opening of the ground separating the two floors, in the form of a screen that bodies can see from either floor. PATRICK BALDWIN

it will be to explore appearance, disappearance and the transition from one to the other.

In addition to using flexible materials and multiples of devices for entrances and exits, the white model should be malleable in terms of secondary three-dimensional forms: duplicates of, and variations on, the various component of the design should be prepared in advance. In this way, each component can easily be augmented or reduced in quantity and quality (size, shape, weight, etc.).

Similarly, a multiplicity of scale figures may also be essential in ensuring as many improvisational options as possible. Again, these do not need to be coloured, they may be best white. They also do not need to be realistically detailed. They can be quite abstract, as long as the human form is still legible so as to help us understand scale. To this end, readymade/industrially produced scale figures found in art shops can be used, as these are clearly identifiable and white. But if we are dealing with more creative types of kinetic bodies, we are better off making our own scale figures from scratch, so as to be able to evoke the creative motion of the body. Scale figures can be rapidly made using card, wires, clay, wax or polymorph.

IMPROVISING WITH MODELS

There are many aspects of a model that can be used for improvisation. But in all cases, the conditions in which the model will be used for improvisation must be carefully considered. Like real-scale improvisation, a range of environmental conditions will constitute the framework within which a certain array of improvisation is possible. For improvisation with scale models, the following conditions should be attended to:

- The space in which the model is located: not only the physical environment, but also the space existing between the model and the environment, i.e. the space that we physically inhabit to play with the model. Should we have access to the model from a particular angle only or from all around? At which level should the model be positioned? Do we need to have access to the model from above and/or from underneath? And so on.
- The way the model is illuminated while improvising with it has significant implications on how well we can evaluate the success of the experiments. For a start, it is essential that our bodies do not cast too much shade on the model whilst we are interacting with it. So, lighting the model may require more than simply using the existing light of the space or positioning a domestic lamp above it. Various lamps positioned all around the model at various heights and angles will ensure the model remains illuminated whilst working on and around it. Additionally, integrating some lighting from within the model may be considered too, especially if lighting is relevant to the design. All lights should, however, be easily manipulated and moved around. Thus, lighting outside the model may be done with angle-poised lamps, while the lighting integrated in the model may be achieved with mini-spotlights clipped to the model. In sports equipment shops, a range of small LED spotlights can be found at affordable prices.
- Finally, time/duration is a factor that may be considered. How much time is allocated to each experiment? This may be based on the timeframes of pre-existing structures (e.g. a scene or music) or it may be based on a goal that may be achieved more or less rapidly. Framing the experiment in terms of duration can also quite simply be a matter of random experimentation: for instance, we may decide that an action has to be taken to alter the model every 20sec, or that we will repeat a particular action ten times before changing to another action. Rigorous rules of this kind provide a framework for experimentation that may offer surprising results.

To improvise with a model is essentially to manipulate all the possible relations between the components at play in a developing design. Anne Bogart's and Tina Landau's *The Viewpoints Book: A Practical Guide to Viewpoints and Composition* (2005) provides an array of practical considerations for improvisation worth applying to experimentation with models. For instance, they ask us to consider 'what is the full range of possible distances between things?' and 'which groupings suggest an event or emotion, express a dynamic?' (Bogart and Landau 2005: 11) by way of manipulating and rearranging 'patterns', 'density', 'symmetry', 'asymmetry', 'scale', 'perspective' and 'juxtaposition'. Though one particular configuration of the modelled design may be the starting point, exploring variations of that configuration can proceed through a variety of approaches: from simply rearranging components in as many new configurations as possible to replacing components with differently sized versions of them. However, every new arrangement also modifies how bodies will enter, inhabit, travel through and exit the space. Thus, for every new arrangement, scaled figures must also be repositioned. Conversely, we may rearrange the grouping of figures first and then adapt the design components to the new grouping.

Either way, the improvisational work is not simply a search for variations of the design, but also an exploration of its dramaturgical potential.

Underwater scale model by Wenjiao Wang depicting set and costume designs for Shakespeare's *A Midsummer Night's Dream* (1605). This is a speculative design for an enormous scenic environment that is mostly aquatic and making use of inks dispersed in water as the magic forces involved in the plot.

Indeed, as entrances and exits are shuffled around, displacing the figures with them, the meaning of the body's position in space may shift. To avoid getting lost dramaturgically, it is often worth considering whether the material and physical approach to improvisation itself should be framed by key themes in the project. Improvisation with a model can be highly performative, wherein our active relationship to the model is predicated on specific physical and dramaturgical conditions. In this sense, we may consider our own subjectivity and physicality as a framework or narrative to drive the improvisation. For instance, in a dramaturgical context where magical forces are concerned, we may decide to devise a magical relationship between ourselves and the model: since magic revolves around the idea of forces beyond human control, a magical relationship to a model may involve setting up material conditions by which we can no longer control the model's variations but instead have it be affected by elements that we can introduce but not control.

Improvisation with the white model is about experimenting with a scaled-down three-dimensional world understood as a dynamic, transformative and transient volume of space. These spatial qualities refer to bodily qualities, as indeed they must be directly relevant to bodies. For this reason, it is useful to approach the model as if it was a body: although it has a quasi-fixed volume, this volume is to be dynamically animated over a certain period of time. Through a scenographic lens, notions such as foreground, midground and background are not fixed: they may be approached as if they were different layers of skins, whereby foreground layers may be shed as back layers come to the fore. We may also consider and explore the location and structure of the 'spine' of the design, as well as its organs and the

Scale model by Oona Tibbets. Multiple LED sources are used to illuminate this model. These are very small and commercially ubiquitous lighting sources that provide light beams almost in scale with the model. Note that the lighting is primarily directed at a large and suspended scenic structure through which it is filtered before reaching the floor in different patterns. Given that the set is dependent on lighting, the inclusion of various sources of light here is absolutely necessary.

circulatory veins and paths created as a result. To approach space as such, an organism highlights the need to conceive of a pulse, a rhythm or what we may call, drawing from Bogart's and Landau's *Viewpoints*, a gesture: 'Gesture is Shape with a beginning, middle and end' (Bogart and Landau 2005: 9). Although they relate gesture to the human body, we can rightfully extend it to artefacts and spaces put into motion. Helpfully, they pinpoint two types of gestures: behavioural and expressive, wherein behavioural gesture is an everyday/known movement and expressive gesture is abstract. This provides us with the two ends of a gestural or kinetic spectrum from which we might draw a range of rhythms to apply to the movement of the model's components.

One component that is invariably helpful in exploring spatial dynamics is light. Even if light is not an actual element of the design, the lighting conditions to which the model is subjected will affect our perception and evaluation of the spatial dynamic at play. As a result, lighting must be carefully arranged on the model, paying particular attention to the positions, angles, directions and distances of the light sources to the various areas of the model. Cutting slits all around the box, or constructing bridges across the top of the box, provides multiple points of fixtures for light sources to be clipped on.

STORYBOARDING WITH MODELS

Since it can easily be recorded in film and photography, the dynamic function of the model can be used for the purpose of composition, as a storyboard. This requires a rather mixed-media approach to both model and storyboarding: the cells of the storyboard may, for instance, be created via photographic documentation of the model, thus in return the model must be prepared for the medium of photography. This means that lighting the model is likely to be adjusted for the camera, while the camera needs to be set to the conditions of the model (small scale requiring a zoom and lighting conditions usually requiring precise exposure). A controlled environment is rather essential for such tasks, as it is important that environmental lighting outside the model is minimized to quasi-darkness. Ideally, the photographic recording of a model for the purpose of creating a storyboard should be done in a dark environment. Photographic storyboards of this kind may enable a more precise depiction of scenes and moments of the design. As such, photographic close-ups should be juxtaposed with larger views of the model whenever we want the focus of a moment to be narrowed down to a particular area.

Although their fixed format does not allow for much rendering of transitions and time, it is possible to extend the photographic record into a

RIGHT: Scale model (overview) for Anton Chekhov's *Three Sisters* (1900) by I-Shun Lee. In this design, the space is split in two areas by a large glass panel on which water is dripping. Bodies are located on either side and relate to, as well as communicate with, each other. Due to the complexity of this visual situation, it is important here to storyboard audience viewpoints, starting with the ideal perspective, which is generally a frontal overview.

overleaf: Scale model (side and close up view) for Anton Chekhov's *Three Sisters* (1900) by I-Shun Lee. A side and close up view on this model is also relevant to capture in order to ensure that all audiences can properly perceive the two scenic areas and their relation in this design.

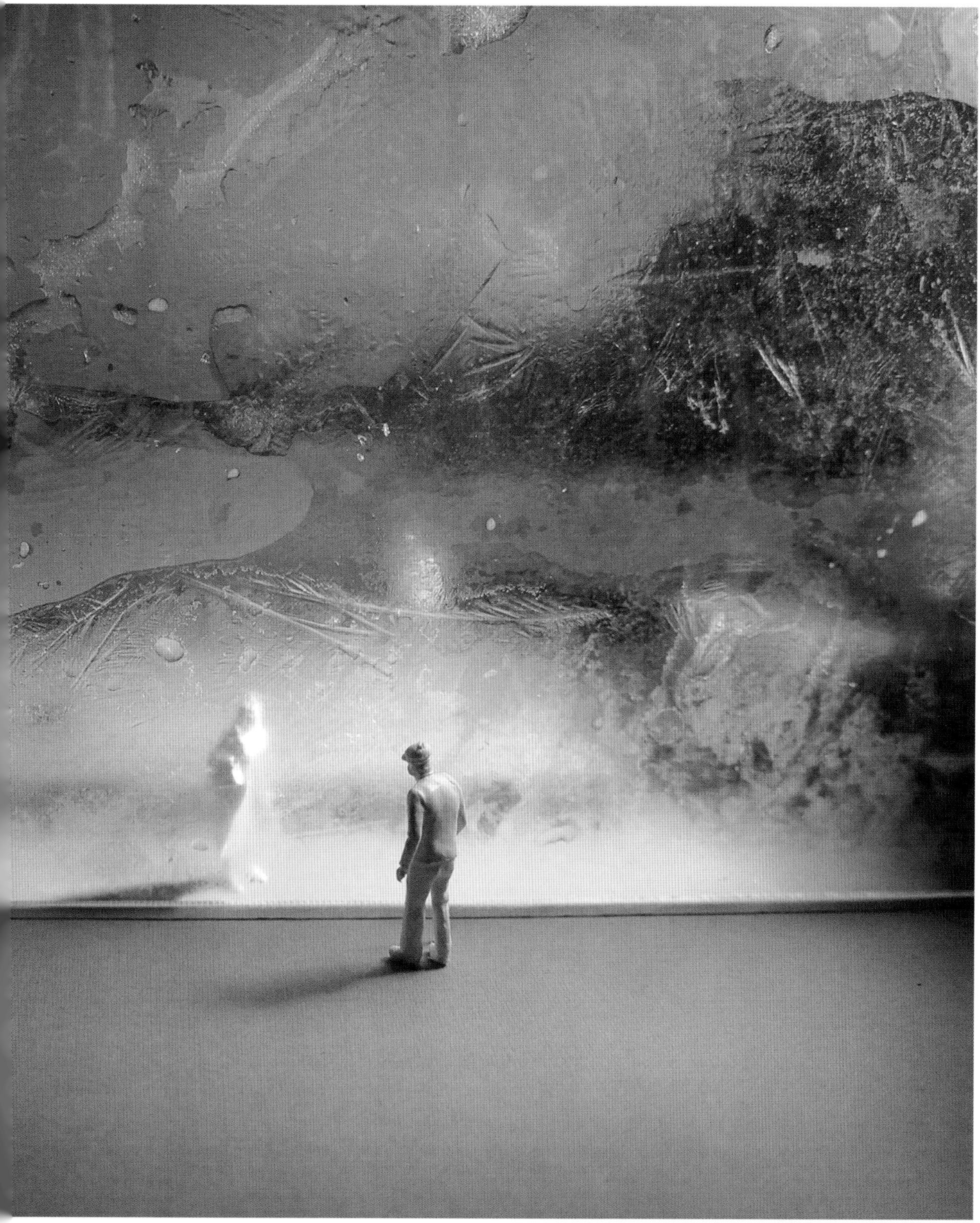

48 MODELLING

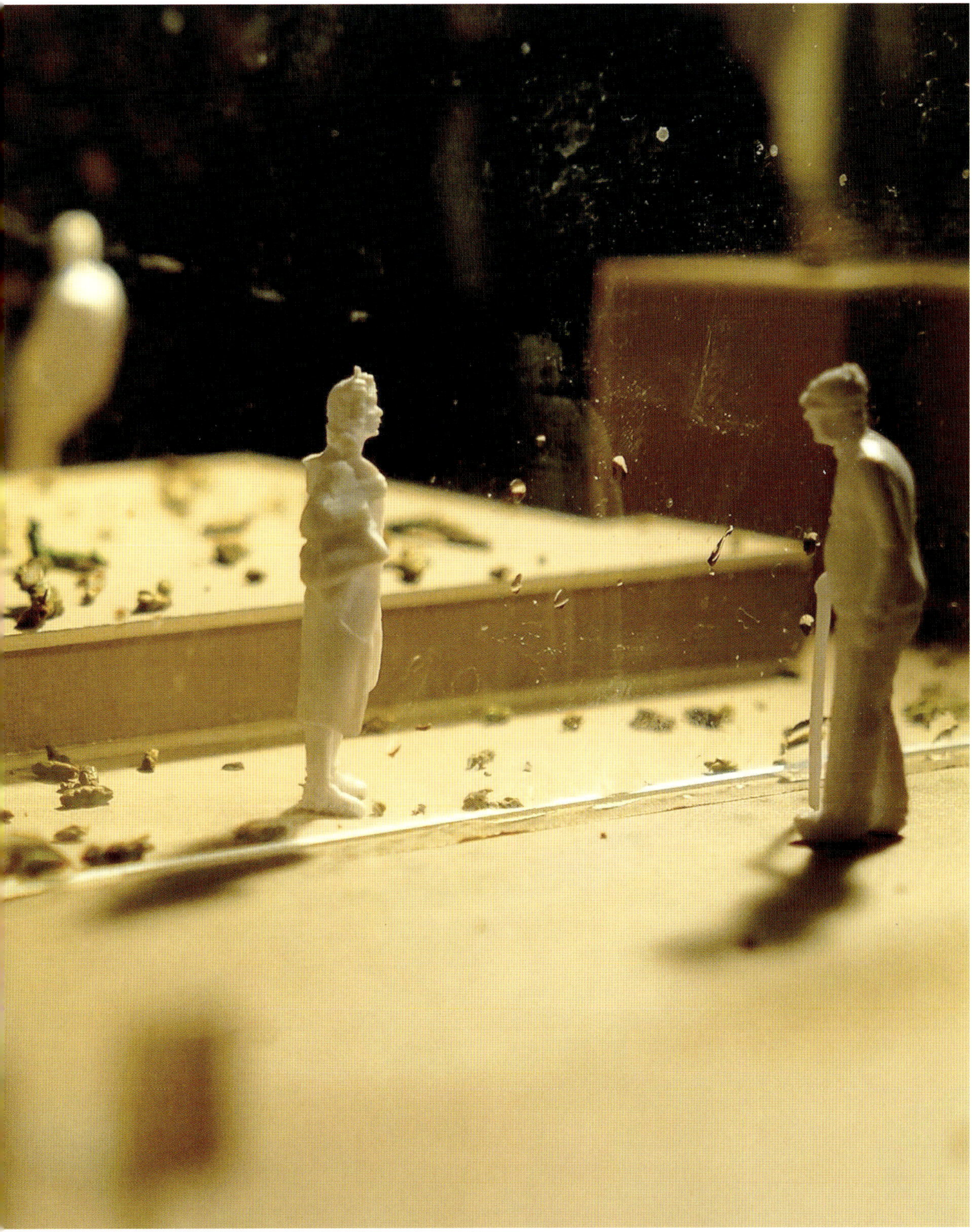

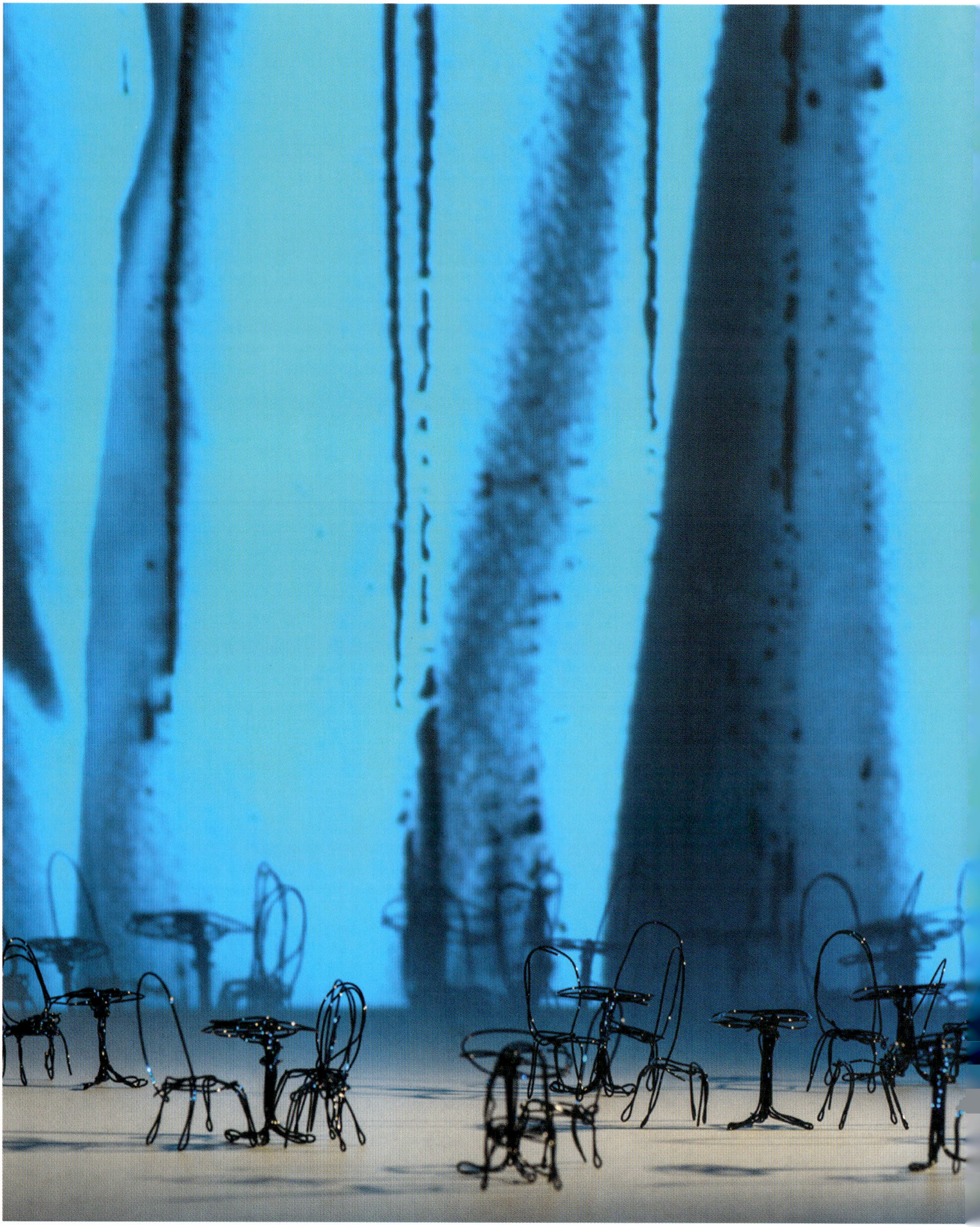

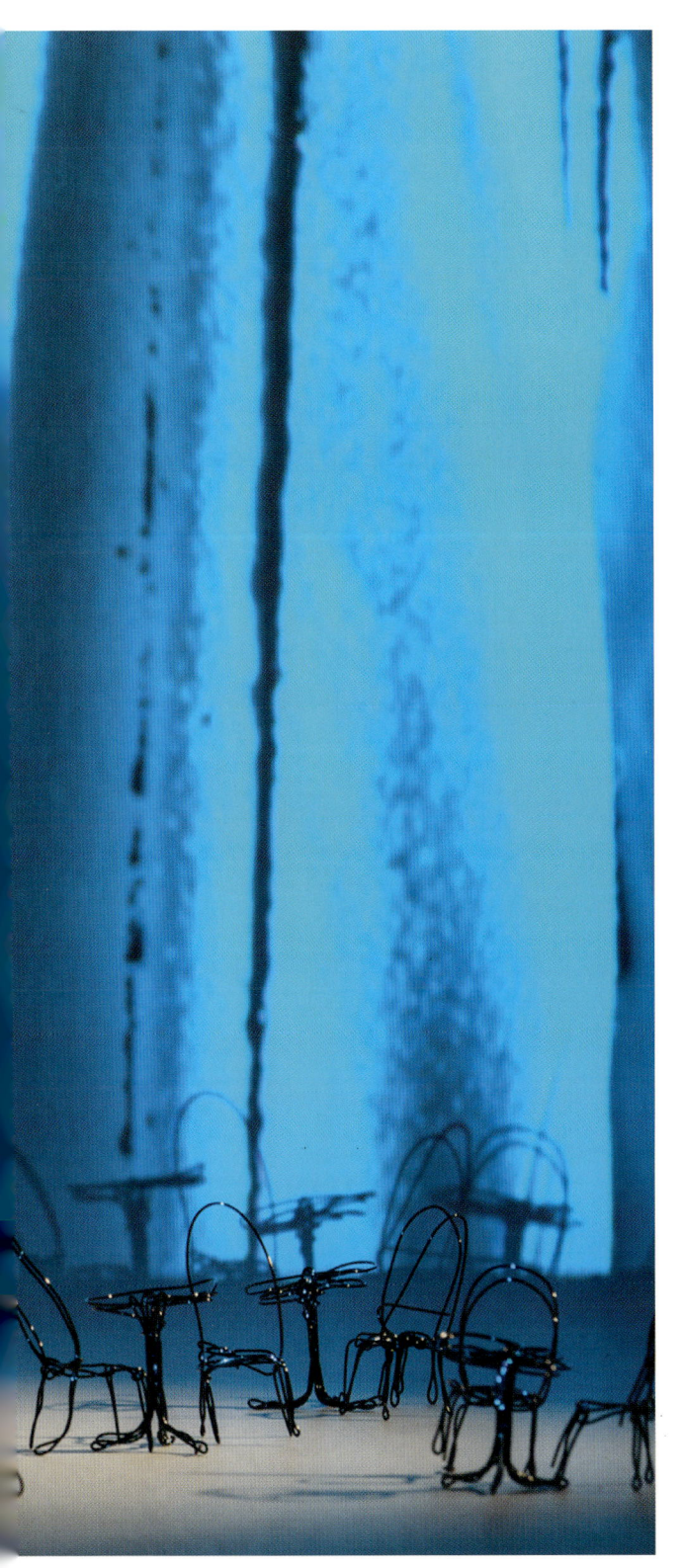

filmic media, i.e. time-based/moving image structure that is necessary to render transitions, transformations from one visual structure to another. If we move the various elements of the model in small increments between individual photographed frames, we can create a strong sense of kinesis and time when the series of frames is edited and played as a continuous film sequence. This is called stop motion and though it is a time-consuming practice, it is very helpful in order to put our minds into details that relate to time. Indeed, because the photographic records are now embedded in a filmic structure, sound can be included in the storyboard to further define the sense of pace, time and progression. Thus, lastly, storyboarding by modelling and recording in stop motion allows for a range of mixed-media experiments, such as the inclusion of projection, which may be physically integrated into the model via pocket projectors or superimposed over the captured frames in post-production editing. It must be pointed out here that the photographic/filmic recording of a projected image (in a model or in any situation) brings about certain challenges, such as frame rates: the pocket projector will be projecting images at a particular frame rate, which is likely to be different from the frame rate of the camera capturing the image. This discrepancy results in shaded horizontal stripes rapidly flickering through the image. In the small-scale space of the model, this distortion is likely to be blatant and detrimental to the overall image. However, this can be simply solved by adjusting the frame rate of the camera

LEFT: Speculative model with projection by Erica Lopes. A mini- or pico-projector can be used in a model to explore the visual interaction between scenery and projection.
PATRICK BALDWIN

OVERLEAF: Physical scale model by Magdalena Iwanska depicting a final scenic design for Botho Strauss' *The Park* (1983). The physical model is particularly useful for communicating some visual components such as colours (especially the juxtaposition of colours in scenery and costumes) but also for the purpose of positioning figures and the various ways in which they can inhabit the space.

52 MODELLING

MODELLING 53

54 MODELLING

to a similar level as the one of the projector. Once both machines have the same frame rate, the projected image will appear, on film, exactly as it does in reality.

Whether photographic or filmic, models can be refined with digital tools and software. In addition to making the modelling process more rapid, digital media enable us to further define details (both aesthetic and technical). In particular, details to do with construction (such as the internal structures of artefacts) can be precisely included in a digital model. However, whereas the technical details of the design may be fully and precisely established in a digital model, the aesthetic dimension of the model can never be fully accurate. Some notable distortions occur due to the digital nature of the medium:

- Perspectival distortions: digital models are created with respect to a structure of linear perspective (with a vantage point), which is a system of representation different from how we physically perceive. As a result, the perspectival representation of depth is only an approximation or stylization of how we actually see three-dimensionality.
- Colour distortions: digital imagery is essentially made of light, thus its primary colours are RGB (red, green and blue); physical colours (such as paints, inks and the colours of materials, objects and substances) have RYB (red, yellow and blue) as primary colours. We thus have two distinct colour wheels wherein their mix (when coloured light hits coloured objects) will provide different results in reality than they do in a digital model. Furthermore, digital colours may quite simply not be quite exactly the same as their counterpart in paint or ink, for instance.

LEFT: Digital scale model by Magdalena Iwanska depicting a final scenic design for Botho Strauss' *The Park* (1983). The model is specifically useful in rendering scenery with precision, which will inform the drafting of technical and construction plans. However, compared to its physical counterpart, the digital nature of this model alters the colours a little and distorts the perception of depth.

TIP FOR USING SCALE MODELS TO DRAW TECHNICAL PLANS

Moving from a physical scale model to its technical rendering and plans can be done digitally but this can be quite a challenging leap. To produce technical drawings for the position, form and dimensions of a spatial structure, one of the most efficient ways is to transfer a physical scale model on a two-dimensional sheet of paper.

1. When you have decided on the preferred and exact positions of a scale model of a spatial structure, slip a sheet of paper right under it, reposition the model if this has displaced it a bit and draw on the paper following the edges of your model. This will provide you with an initial ground plan of the same scale as your model was and which you can then further detail by inscribing all the relevant dimensions.

2. On a new sheet of paper, place your scale model structure as it would stand in your model box, draw all around it edges to produce a top view, then gently get hold of the two ends of the model, flip it horizontally so that its back lies against the paper and lower it around 5cm underneath the drawn top view (ensuring the two opposite ends of your model are aligned on paper with the two opposite ends drawn in the top view). Now draw again on the paper following the edges of the model. You now have a front view. Finally, hold the two opposite ends of the model again, raise the right-hand side up until the model stands on its left side, drag it around 5cm to the left of the front view drawing, ensuring that the top and bottom ends of the drawing and the model stay aligned on paper, and again draw around the edges of the model. You have now produced a left-side view. You may repeat the same step for the right-side view. You have now created the outlines of an orthographic rendering of your spatial structure. It is very likely that you still need to complete this rendering by drawing additional components and details within these outlines. For this, measure these elements, as well as their distances and angles, to key points of the model edges. Then identify where these key points are located on your drawn outlines, and use these measurements to draw in these additional details.

PROFESSIONAL INSIGHT

MODEL-MAKING
Yoon Bae

Yoon Bae is a set and costume designer and a teaching professional in the United Kingdom and the USA. Her theatre and opera designs have been shown internationally, including in Japan, Korea, United Kingdom, USA and Norway. She won Best Set Design (San Francisco Bay Area Theatre Critics Award) for Disconnect and Best Set and Costume Award (Arizona Republic) for The Importance of Being Earnest.

Over the years I have discovered and deployed many shortcuts and cheats to help my design process flow. These tips will help you improvise with your tools and enhance the clarity of your modelled designs.

Scale

If you don't have a scale ruler to hand, you can use this quick tip to measure. So, for example, if the space is 10m deep, in reality that equates to 400mm on your 1:1 ruler in 1:25 scale.

If you are working in America, the units change from metric (centimetres and meters) to imperial (feet and inches) and the scale changes accordingly. A quarter inch (¼in) and a half-inch (½in) architecture scales are commonly used in the U.S. The ¼in scale means a quarter inch equates to one foot and zero inches. It is written down as: ¼in = 1in–0in. Therefore ½in scale is noted as ½in= 1in–0in. In this scale a half inch equates to one foot.

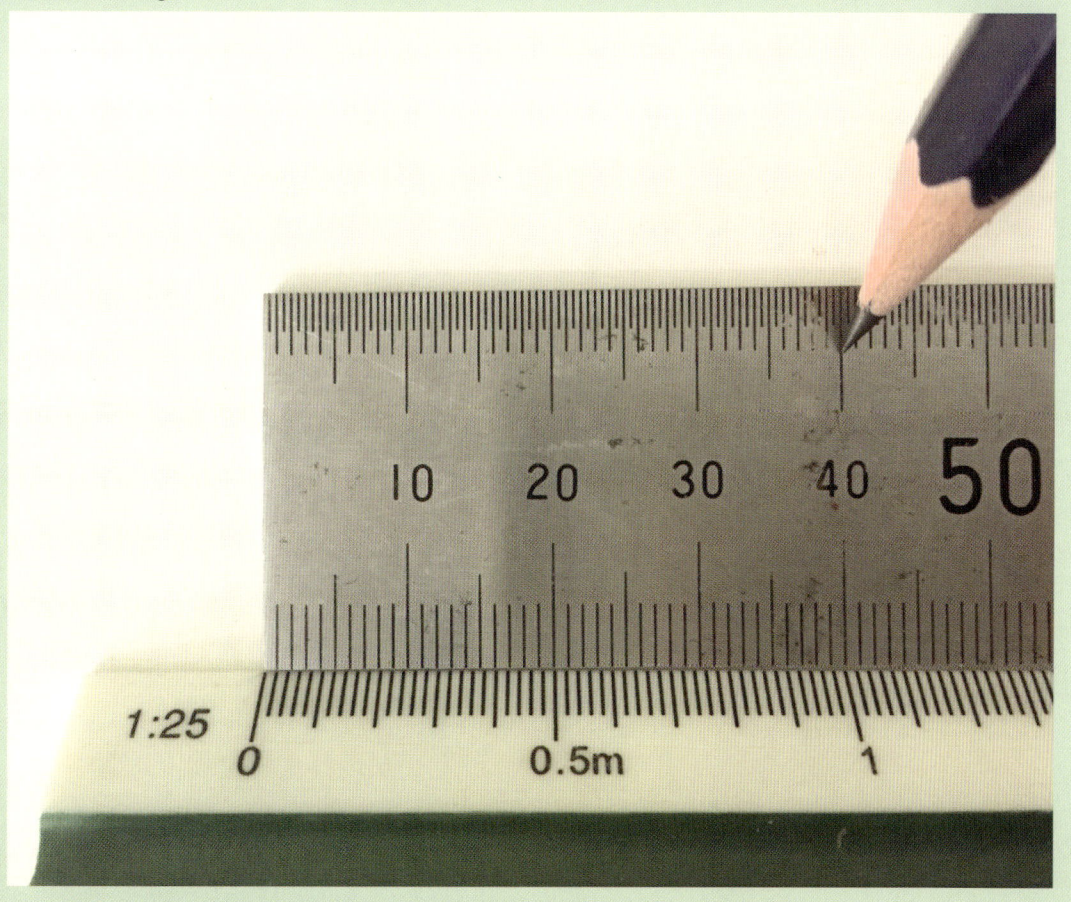

4cm on a 1:1 scale ruler is the same as 1m in 1:25 scale.

(*continued overleaf*)

(*continued from previous page*)

Circle
If you don't have a compass and you need to draw a circle, it is easy to use paper and two sharp pencils to draw a neat circle.

Done! You now have a perfect circle at your required size.

For smaller circles: the dimension of a hole punch circle is 150mm diameter in 1:25 scale. Use the cut-out circles for lots of small circles in model-making. Paint the paper or use colour paper when punching holes.

Weight
A one penny coin gives enough weight for most tall model pieces (and people) to stand securely upright in your model box. Alternatively, you can buy a bag of washers. The weight and size of the penny, for me, has always been just right.

First, decide the radius and measure and draw that line on a piece of paper.

Next, using your sharpened pencils, puncture two holes in the paper at either end of the radius line you have just drawn.

Then, keeping the pencils in the holes, place one pencil at the centre of your required circle on the drafting paper (do not lift the pencil until the circle is complete) and begin to draw the circumference with the other pencil.

Floor lamp weighted down by a one-penny coin.

(continued overleaf)

(continued from previous page)

Stairs

'Riser' is the vertical section of a step, and the 'tread' is the horizontal section.

'Going' is measured from nosing to nosing.

'Riser' is measured between the top surfaces of the treads.

Divide the height from the bottom level to the top of the next level by a predetermined height of your choice for the riser. Remember, you don't have to walk it but an actor does.

A rise between 150mm and 220mm is normal and the going is usually between 220mm and 300mm. Generally, if the minimum rise and minimum going are used the steps will be too narrow, and if the maximum rise and maximum going are used the steps will be tall and deep. Thus the common relationship between the dimensions of the rise and going is twice the rise plus the going, and should be kept within a range of 550mm to 700mm (2R + G = 550mm and 700mm). This is a standard industry equation that doesn't quite mathematically work. However, these are the parameters for staircase calculation from which you can interpret and create your design. A comfortable staircase angle is about 30°- 35°. The staircase angle can be more flexible for a stage set but remember that any angle lower than 20° is too low and a staircase angle over 50° is too steep and dangerous to walk. This is a basic staircase calculation guide, which can vary depending on the needs of your design.

Staircases are difficult to model in scale. They are a nightmare to build quickly and when you are at the exploring stage it is a waste of time to build multiple staircases while you discover what works. The easy way around this is to print technical drawings of a staircase and cut them out – you can adjust the configuration and print again until you feel it is right.

When it is time to turn your drawings into your final model piece, using toothpicks for banisters takes a bit more time but looks so much better.

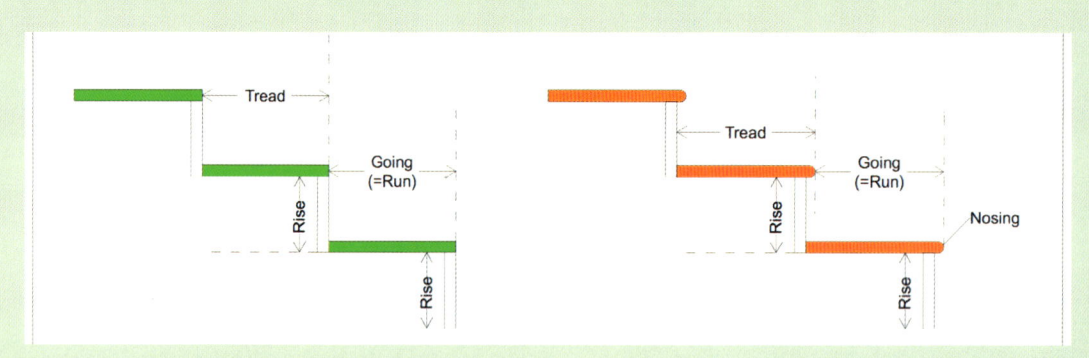

Stair without nosing and stair with nosing.

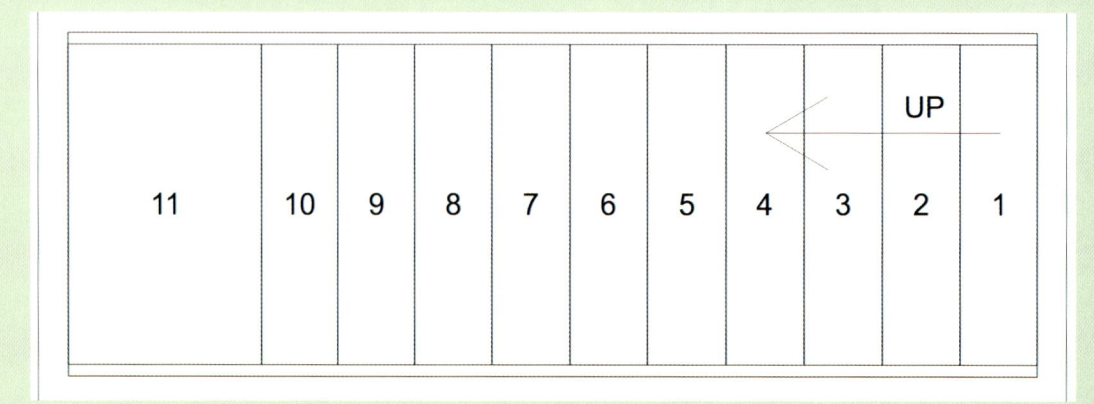

Technical drawing of staircase, top view.

Technical drawing of staircase, front elevation.

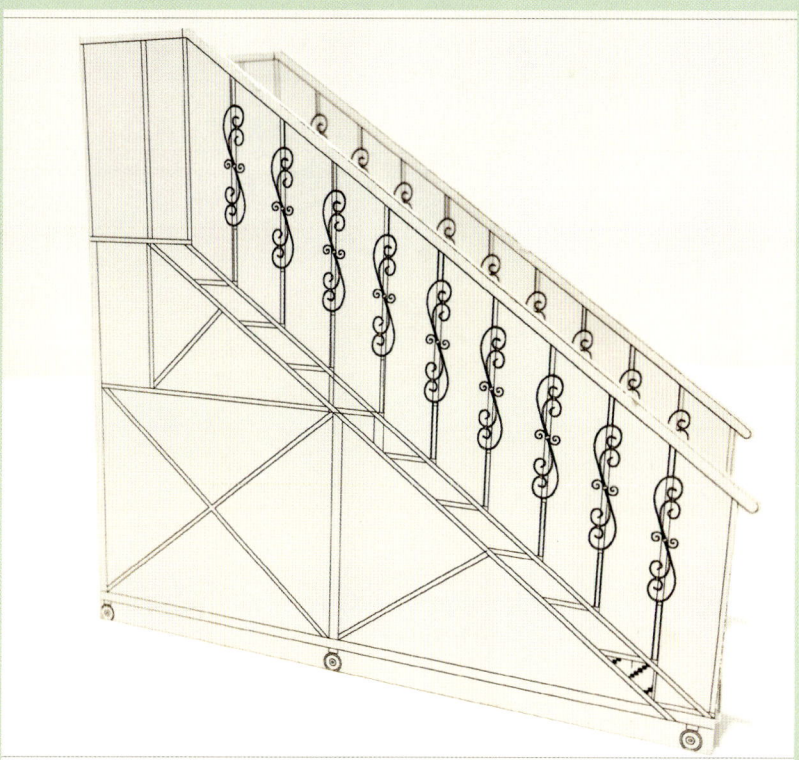

Model of staircase, front view.

(continued overleaf)

(continued from previous page)

Model of staircase, rotated angle.

Banisters.

Lighting
Use the torch (flash) on your mobile phone or any single beam light to see the effect of light on your model. A Maglite has a beam you can focus and move around to see and play with light effects on your model. You can also put coloured gel samples over the beam to explore the effect of colours.

Without directional light.

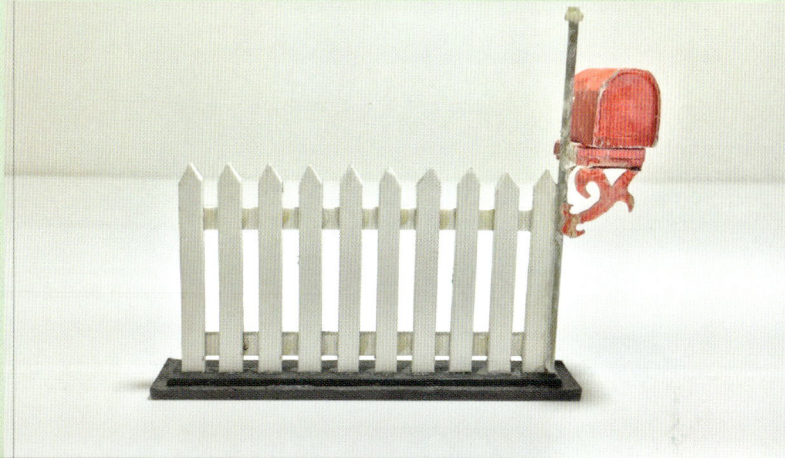

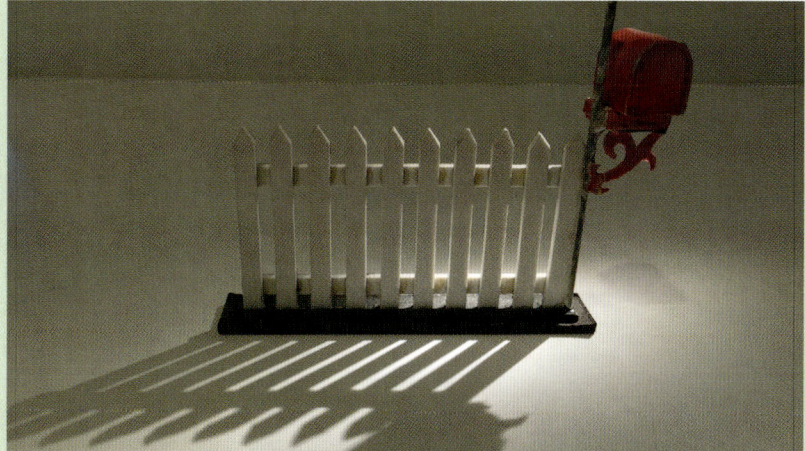

With directional light.

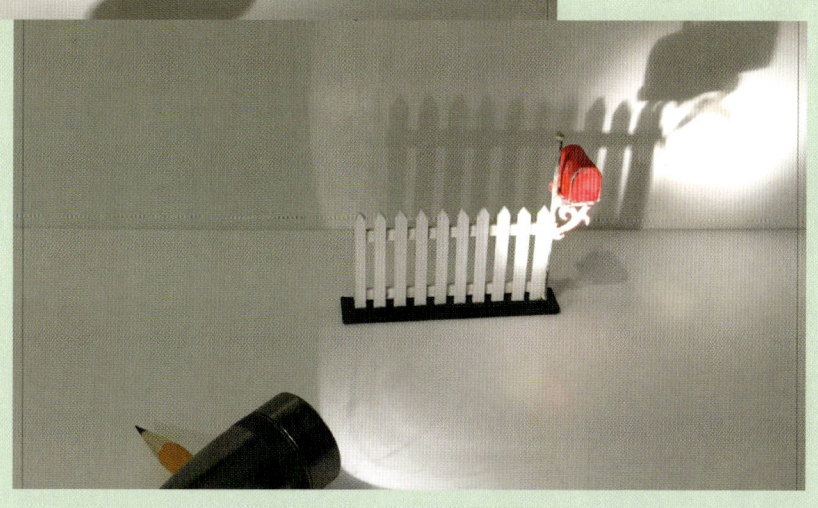

Torch setting.

(continued from previous page)

Curve
To create curved walls or round columns, score the back of the paper (mount board or foam board) lightly at regular intervals. If you score too lightly, the paper will not curve, but if scored too hard, the paper will be cut through. Test the perfect scoring depth and distance between the scoring lines.

Moving from one ruler placement to the next to score a vertical line takes time; you can speed this up by using a set square.

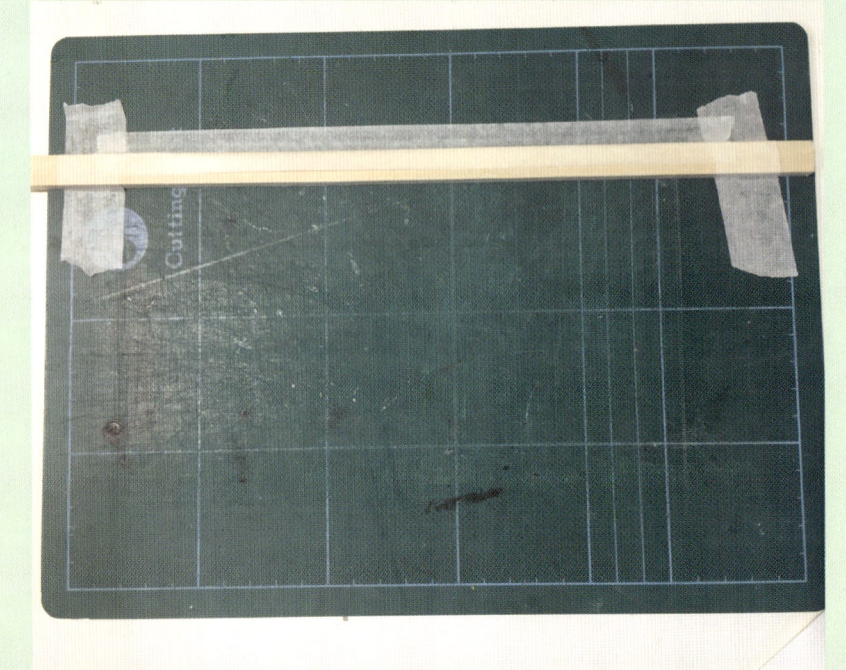

If you don't have a set square handy, tape down a wooden stick to your cutting mat (use the grid lines on your cutting mat to set it parallel).

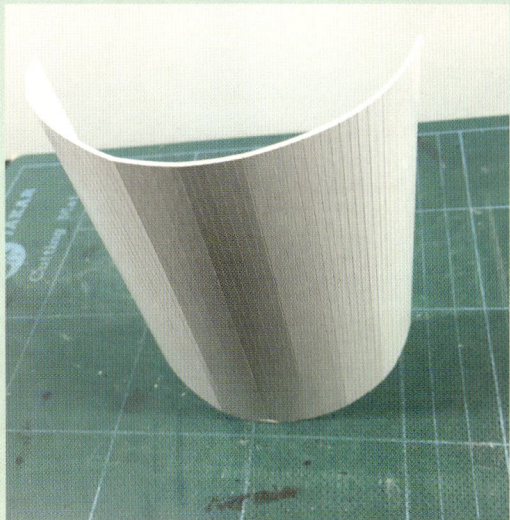

ABOVE LEFT: Make sure the top edge of your steel ruler glides against the wood stick. In this way you create vertical lines quickly.

ABOVE RIGHT: Once the full length is scored, curve the paper...

RIGHT: ...then join the ends together.

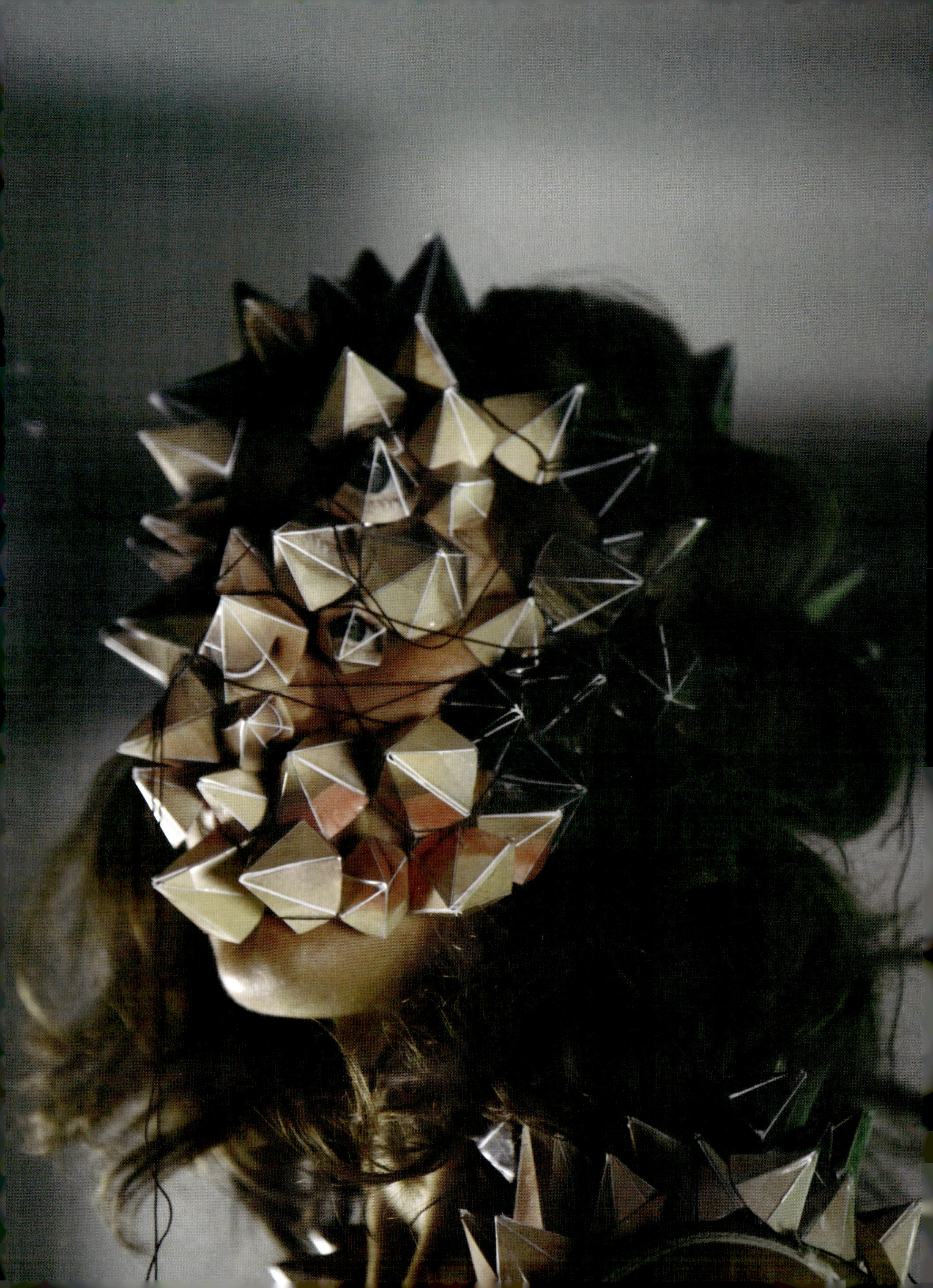

3
PROTOTYPING

The transition from conception to realization within a creative process often involves some form of testing through prototyping. To a certain extent, models may be considered as scaled prototypes. However, in this chapter, prototyping is understood as any real-scale artefact or experiment made as a mock-up. We will look at prototyping with objects, spaces, phenomena and bodies. Indeed, through prototyping we test out certain parameters related to actual materials, structures, bodies, spaces and time. The purpose of prototyping and testing may be very precise, such as evaluating the robustness of a material, or much more experimental wherein the prototype is used for improvisation in order to find out what it can do or enable. Prototyping may, therefore, be used for both creative development and technical feasibility.

Either way, prototyping requires and expands our practical understanding of material and technical properties. Here conception is moving towards realization. Even if the making part is undertaken by a construction specialist, it is essential for the creative author to understand processes of construction and materials. These will allow you to anticipate feasibility, as well as to engage in creative collaboration with constructors.

A prototype ideally goes through three phases: it is first roughly mocked up to define its form, then a provisional artefact is constructed to test out its use and function, then a final version of the artefact is realized and finalized aesthetically. This chapter discusses effective ways of engaging with each of these three phases.

OPPOSITE: *Prosthetic Gods* by Dallas Wexler. JEMIMA YONG

PREPARATION FOR PROTOTYPING

When the phase of creative conception has reached rather specific designs, it is often the case that components of these designs will raise questions and problems: these may be very practical issues to do with feasibility (such as construction, safety or longevity) or aesthetic concerns (such as proportions, spacing, forms and colours). Because there are costs associated with prototyping, it is much considered in relation to practical feasibility. Although the creative problem-solving of both practical and aesthetic problems allows creative engagement and development, it is useful to approach and undertake each type of prototyping separately. Indeed, to start with, we might not invite the same collaborators for both types: typically, a technical/production team is essential to prototyping for technical feasibility, whereas the creative team is more relevant to involve in creative prototyping (or it may even be undertaken individually). Thus, when the need to mock-up and test out emerges, it is important to identify the right collaborators to contribute to the testing.

To start off the process of prototyping, an initial mock-up is constructed to define the shape and size of the prototype that will then be realized for testing. Such a mock-up tends to be made of cheap materials that stand in for the actual materials that will be used in the next phase. Off-cuts and other waste materials can be sufficient to construct this initial artefact (as well as glue and

Mock-up shoes by Tong Zhao. This is an initial prototype made of scraps of plastic bottles, card and paper. The sole purpose of this prototype is to mock-up the unusual shape and proportions of these shoes.

pins to assemble its parts), since the construction techniques required for the final artefact do not need to be implemented yet. This mock-up is only a preparatory artefact that will serve as the basis for realizing the prototype for testing.

Sometimes a mock-up is made as a stand-in for a series of similar artefacts. The variations on this artefact may not require each to be prototyped. Therefore, only one will be made, but its construction will need to be done so that it can be constructed again slightly differently. A rendering of these variations is then relevant to produce before constructing a mock-up. In this way, we can ensure that the construction technique required for that prototype will be expedient with the other related artefacts. Such rendering might be more or less detailed, depending on what actually varies from artefact to artefact. Again, like the initial mock-up, this type of sketch is tentative and not yet a technical rendering.

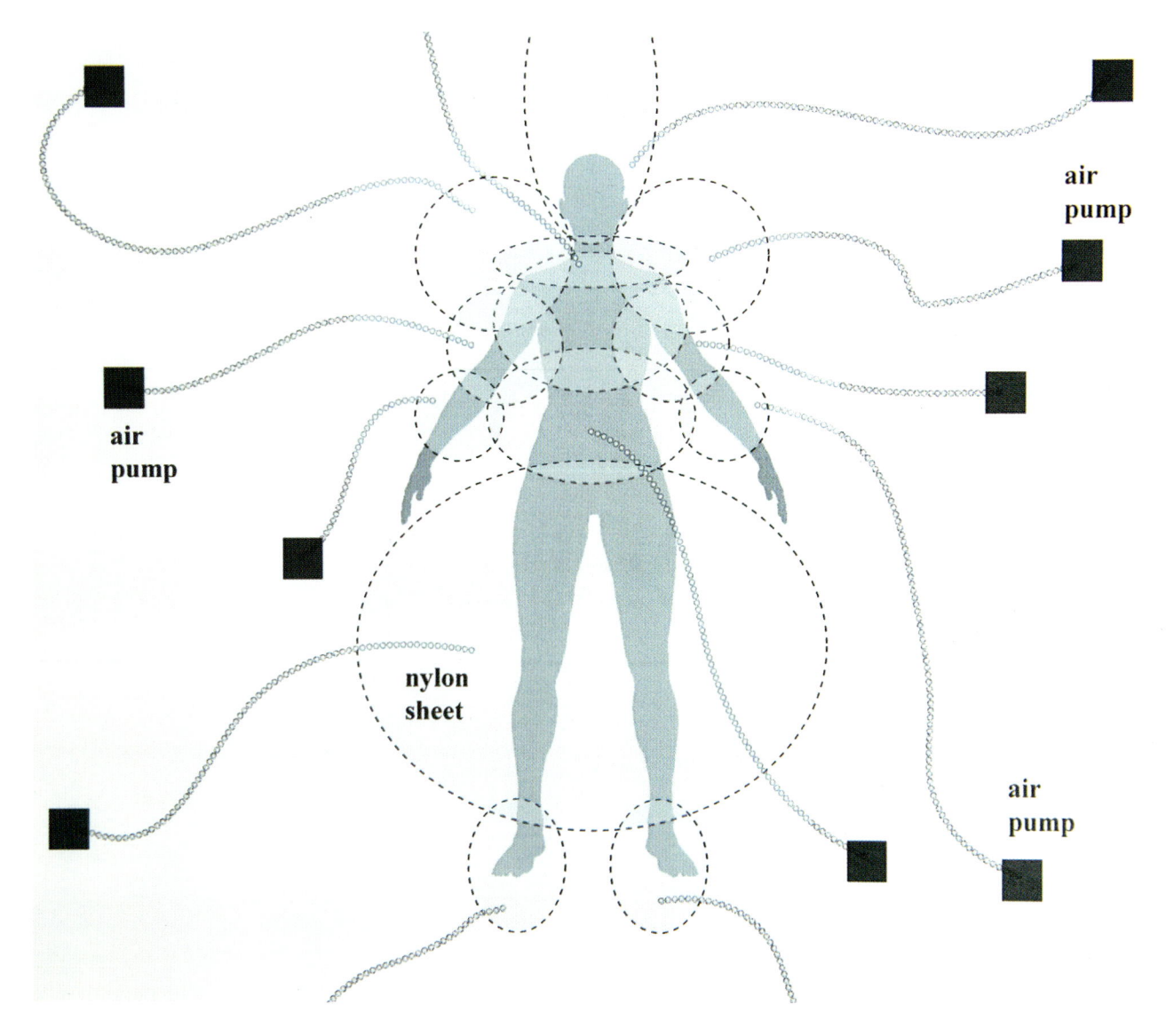

Diagram for prototyping by Meni Kourmpeti. This schematic drawing shows a plan for multiple similar prosthetic artefacts to be prototyped in relation to various areas of the body. Such a diagram is helpful in either anticipating the full scope of prototyping to come, which will inform the choice of materials and ways to prototype the very first artefact to test out, or speculating on the further developments of a tested prototype.

MATERIALS

Based on an initial mock-up, a prototype for testing can be constructed. To do so, we must not only have some pre-existing idea of its form and function, but also of the possible materials to test out. Terms like wood, metal or plastic are families of materials within which many different kinds of materials and properties can be found. Therefore, it is insufficient to conceive of a prototype simply made of wood or metal or plastic. Which wood? Which metal? Which plastic? These are crucial questions because there are more and more types of wood, metal and plastic. In addition, an increasing amount of composite materials are created.

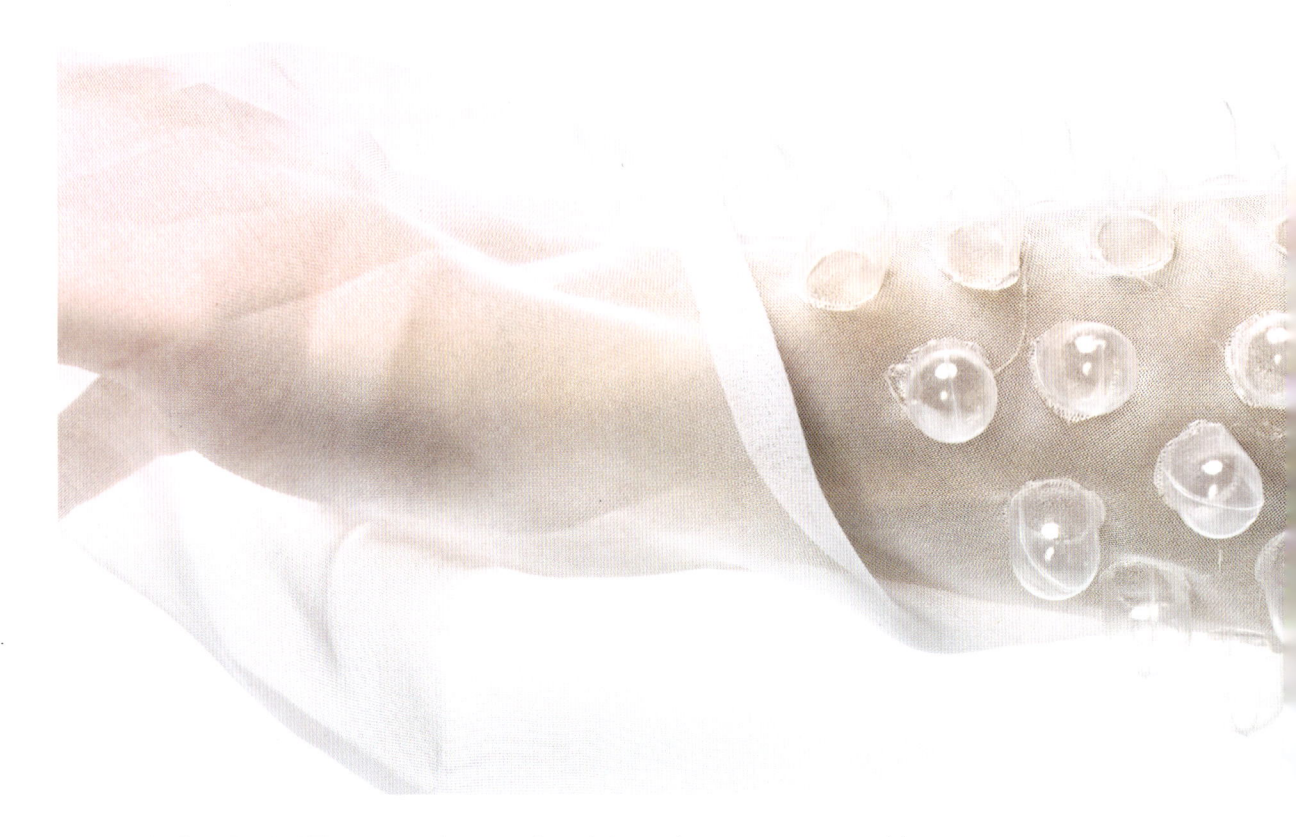

Prototype by Sofia Esquivel. The prototype is an experiment in integrating two common materials together to create an unusual composite material, surface and texture. THOMAS FARMER

Thus, this is not a matter of deciding between iron and aluminium, but of understanding the different existing types of iron and aluminium, and the further treatments and properties these materials take on. The appearance of the prototype may need to be that of aluminium but this does not force us to use aluminium since there are plastic materials that imitate aluminium perfectly, such as mirrorized polyester films and metallic acrylics.

Knowledge of materials comes through researching and contacting retailers and manufacturers to obtain samples and technical specifications. Now, of course, no technical specification will ever include a complete list of how materials interact with other materials. Material interactions can be unpredictable and, therefore, usually requires prototyping. In this case testing is done through the making of the prototype itself. For instance, to create a fabric that has plastic properties and textures, we might want to explore ways of attaching plastic elements to a fabric; in other words, experimenting with how fabric and plastic materials might interact.

By prototyping through experimentation with materials, we obtain material knowledge that might not be found otherwise. Therefore, the precise materials used for, and the findings we obtain from, prototyping are worth recording in a personal material library.

Material knowledge also includes understanding construction processes. This does not necessarily mean proficiency in such processes. If we understand how existing carpentry tools can alter wood, we are more likely to conceive of a wooden prototype that will yield successful results. Even with more recent tools like three-dimensional printers, there are different techniques and materials available that will have different results. Yet again, these processes may be experimented with to produce surprising new results. The use and misuse of these known materials and tools together constitutes the basis for a personal and thorough knowledge of materials.

TESTING

Prototypes are meant to be tested, since they are 'constructed from the materials of problem situations which are puzzling, troubling, and uncertain' (Schön 1983: 40). In the context of prototyping for creative developments, testing is what Donald Schön calls 'problem setting'…, 'a process in which, interactively, we name the things to which we will attend and frame the context in which we will attend to them' (Schön 1983: 40). And here again, 'improvisation consists on varying, combining and recombining a set of figures within the schema which bounds and gives coherence to the performance' (Schön 1983: 55). The more combinations are tried out, the more findings will be obtained. Different schemes with different rules can also be experimented with 'to improvise is to follow the ways of the world, as they open up, rather than to recover a chain of connections, from an end point to a starting point, on a route already travelled' (Ingold 2011: 216).

A framework for prototyping is extremely important to guide the conditions under which we interrogate and evaluate a prototype. We may be testing the prototype according to different frameworks that often overlap, but can generally be split into three categories:

- Conceptual framework: where the prototype is tested and evaluated with respect to a discursive inquiry or structure, such as a question, a narrative, a concept or a metaphor.
- Performative framework: where the prototype is tested and evaluated in relation to the body, bodily situations and problems.
- Perceptual framework: where the prototype is tested and evaluated with regards to questions and problems of a sensory and aesthetic nature.

CONCEPTUAL FRAMEWORK

Testing a prototype within a conceptual framework means that we are setting problems of a discursive kind. For instance, Anne Bogart and Tina Landau recommend experimenting with 'spatial metaphors' such as 'I'm up against the wall' or 'lost in space' (Bogart and Landau 2005: 11). In addition to existing metaphors, we can also formulate new discursive problems that may or may not have a solid meaning but still suggest a paradox

Prototype by Chiara La Ferlita. A sample piece of neoprene altered to emulate the textures of both landscape and human skin. The prototype is evaluated on the basis of how effectively it communicates the concept of *skinscape* (hence the photograph's aerial viewpoint). PATRICK BALDWIN

Prototype by Chiara La Ferlita. Another prototype of a *skinscape:* here resin has been moulded on a hand and thus capture its shapes and textures. Does this prototype better communicate the concept? PATRICK BALDWIN

or problem: for instance, we might be interested in the landscape as a skin, or we could call it a *skinscape*, which equally suggests a conundrum that may take various prototypical forms. Though there are similarities between skin and land, the paradox here is related to scale. Like our skin, the land is sculpted by the weather and the movement of the earth underneath. But their scale is extremely different. Conceptually then, a *skinscape* disrupts our common understanding of both skin and landscape as distinct and separate notions. We might then decide to explore how a material surface might be perceived as both skin and landscape. Here prototyping might start with selecting materials that will be altered and manipulated so as to evoke the folds and wrinkles of both landscape and skin. Textiles such as felt and neoprene have a skin-like quality and can be easily altered, folded and textured. Also, resins and silicon can be lightly applied on surfaces to capture their textures (just remember to first coat the surface with oil or Vaseline so as to avoid it sticking to the resin/silicon). Once dried, they can be peeled off and, if using silicon, further manipulated. Evaluation of such prototypes then would revolve around the visual reading they offer – some evoking more clearly the skin and/or the land more than others. Thus, importantly, the prototypes should be observed from a variety of angles, some of which, again, will communicate the concept better than others.

To sum up – when testing a prototype within a conceptual framework: define key notions that encapsulate conceptual problems/shifts; explore material translations of these notions; and evaluate the prototypes by discursive analysis (does this artefact suggest/communicate the key notion?).

PERFORMATIVE FRAMEWORK

Testing a prototype within a performative framework means that we are setting up problems to do with the body. This is quite common in performance design, as many scenery, costumes and props do need to be mocked-up and used by

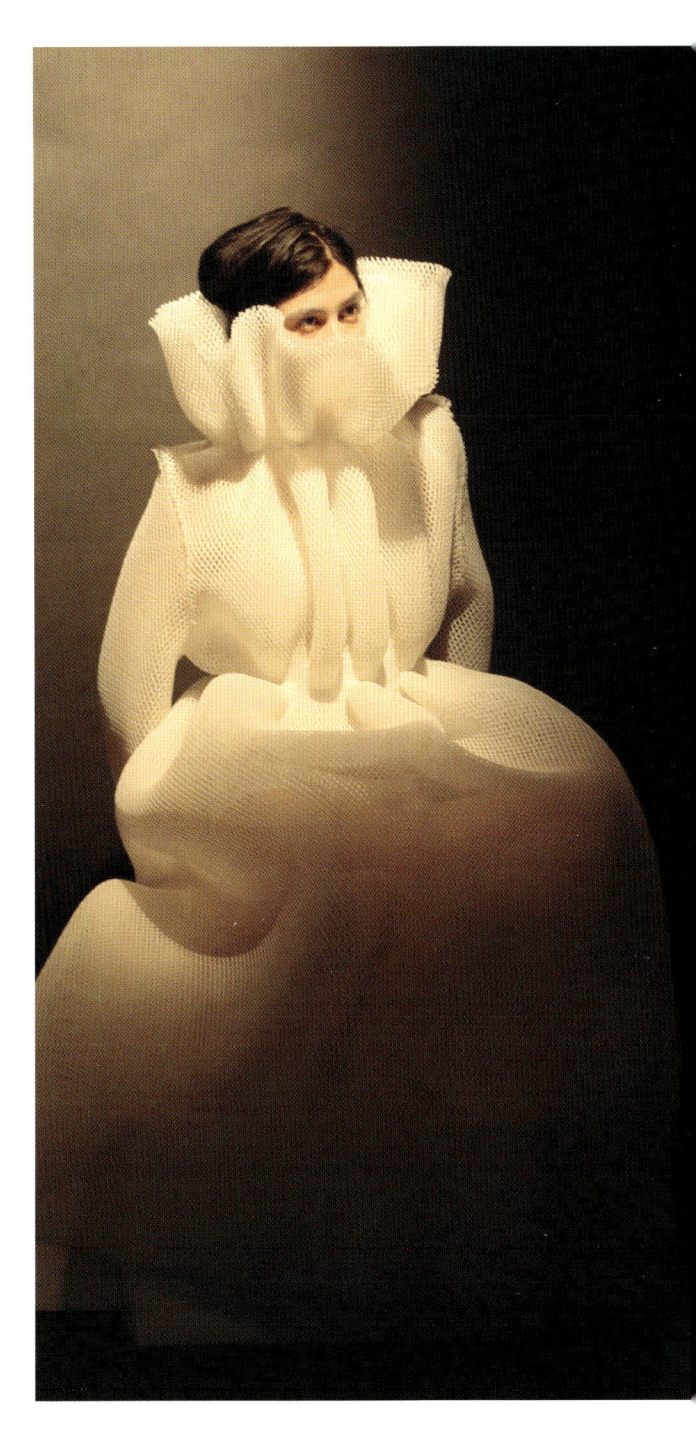

Prototype by Olga Ntenta. This prototype garment includes unusual features that restrict the body wearing it; as such, it is essential that a mock-up is tried out by a performer. Here, this is done in the context of a black box studio, under theatrical lighting, in order to also evaluate the visual properties of the material used in the prototype. JEMIMA YONG

TASKS FOR USING YOUR OWN BODY AS A TOOL FOR IMPROVISATION

Before introducing a prototype artefact to other bodies, you can use your own body as a testing ground for the prototype. In this way, you can anticipate, to some extent, how others might employ and improvise with your prototype. This should happen even before prototyping by way of imagining your body in the place of your audience and the performers, for instance. However, when prototyping, your body should be physically mobilized in relation to the prototype. Simple rules and tasks can be tried out by yourself and, based on the results, replicated with others later on. Here are some tasks you can trial:

1. If your prototype is to meant to be worn, then wear it and try various positions and movements to observe and evaluate how your garment is allowing or restricting movements, as well as how it shifts and folds: stretch your arms up and then move them in a circular motion clockwise and anti-clockwise; bend your whole body forward and backward; sit, kneel down, lie down; walk by making as big steps as you can, jump and run.
2. If your prototype is meant to be hand-held, then explore every way you can to hold this object, and apply light to heavy strength. Observe and evaluate the best areas to grip and hold the artefact; identify the areas that prevent a good grip. Is the object's shape causing problems? Or is it its weight? Or its material surface? Then consider whether some areas of the artefact require resurfacing with a light coating of transparent glue mixed with sand to provide a better grip where the palm of the hand and fingers are best located. Consider whether the artefact needs to be made in a lighter material or whether some areas need to be reshaped. With a permanent pen, mark the areas of the artefact that require alterations. You may also want to test the robustness of the artefact by dropping it on soft and hard floors, at different heights. This will also highlight how the artefact reacts and what that reaction might communicate: for instance, an object made of silicon and painted to look like metal might bounce off the floor and dispel the illusion of metallic substance.
3. When prototyping a spatial structure, you may use some of the above tasks to test how the structure reacts to a body interacting with it. It is also worthwhile testing out the stability of the structure by indirect physical interaction: for instance, you may walk around the structure with more or less heavy steps to evaluate whether the structure starts vibrating as a result. You may repeat this test by placing the structure on a raked or uneven floor to evaluate whether the vibration of your steps on the floor is causing the structure to move. Consider stepping around the structure at various distances.

Keep coming back to your own body and what else it might do to, or around, your prototype.

---

performers before they can be finalized. However, much attention must be paid to how these are tried on. Bringing a prototypical prop for performers to use in a rehearsal context has its hazards. Some guidance may be required as to pointing out to the performers whether there are fragile areas in the prop. Just as importantly, how performers may improvise with the prop is likely to necessitate some guidance. Thus, we may bring some drawings of, or discursively describe, certain images or actions using that prop. Similarly, when it comes to garments, in performance design we have these tried on in wardrobe areas (these are called fittings) where the lighting and environment are different from the stage. As such, the testing of prototype garments should also be done on stage with the correct lighting and surroundings. Moreover, a performance space will enable performers to move a lot more than in a wardrobe, thus putting the costume through appropriate testing of its flexibility.

The more performers are working with materials they have little experience of, the more important their performative testing. This is not only relevant to evaluating the materials' performative potential (what it can and cannot do), but also to test how they endure the passage of time. At the same

PROTOTYPING 75

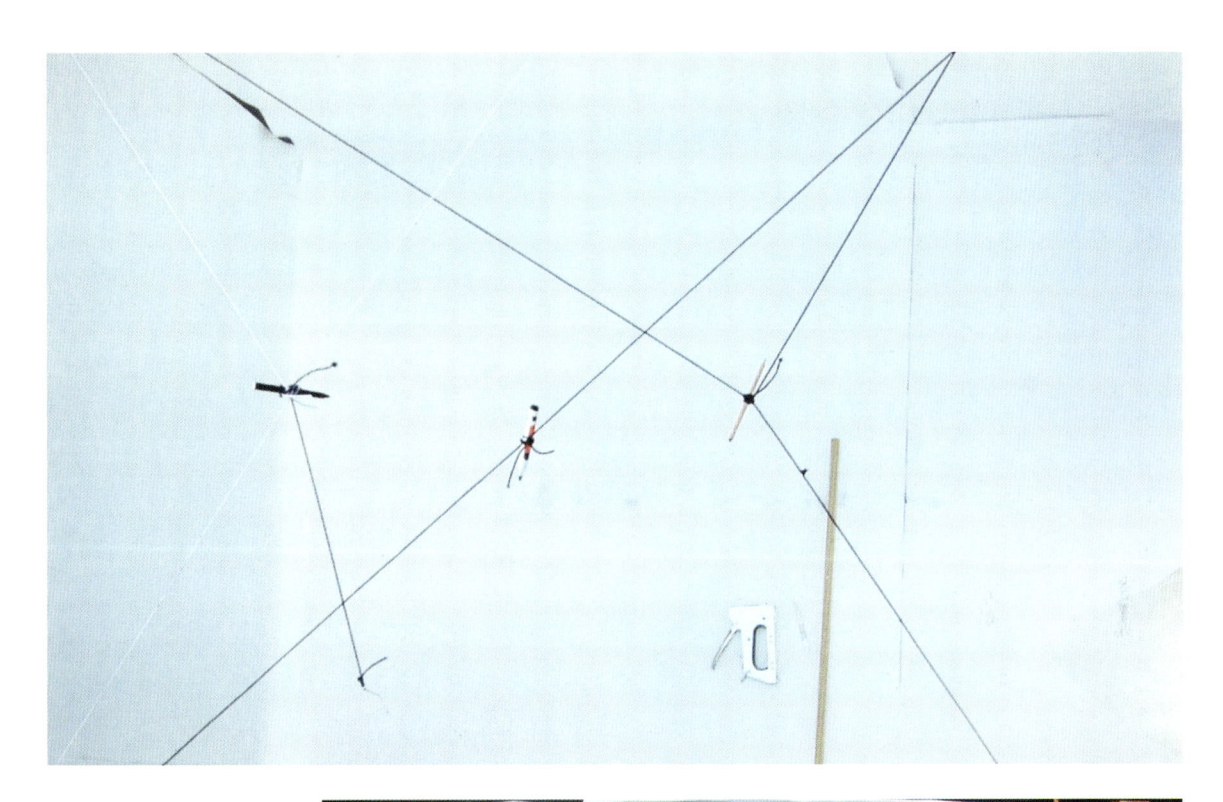

ABOVE: Prototype – set-up, by Lara Farnham. When engaging in performative prototyping, it is useful to document how the practical context for testing has been set up (before the body is included). If successful, the prototype can be more easily replicated as a result.

RIGHT: Prototype – testing, by Lara Farnham. This prototype tests out the interaction of a body and drawing tools attached to elastics in a constructed cube of paper. Here the body itself is being tested, as much as the environmental set-up.

time, besides these functional aspects of performative prototyping, this is again an opportunity for creative development if we open the prototype to improvisation.

Performative improvisation of a scenographic kind is driven by materials, objects and environmental conditions to which the body playfully adapts to some extent as these materials, objects and conditions are also adapted. Thus, both the body and the external stimuli are tested. It is what we might call a relational mode of prototyping, where the body is tentatively conditioned to explore how to relate to its new material situation. For this reason, much material preparation is required to set up performative prototyping. The material situation for the experiment is so determinant, it is

Prototype by Francesc Serra Vila. Here cracks are prototyped by layering plaster over a fabric that is then stretched to cause crackling in the drying coat of plaster. Different stages of the drying plaster and different ways of stretching the fabric will cause a range of cracks, which are then evaluated in terms of their visual legibility.

Prototypes by Emily Pavlatou. Canvas dipped in wax to create a composite material and a new texture changing the perception of textile to that of flesh.

always worth planning it as much as possible and documenting it, as well as the actual performative experiment within it.

The body might not need to be prepared in any way other than by knowing the rules of the experiment. However, these rules may be changed as the performative experiment progresses. As we observe and deem certain actions and phenomena more or less successful, some rules may be cancelled and other rules may be created. Often we repeat the same experiment with slightly different rules to see if it will produce different results. Performers themselves can provide interesting suggestions of new rules based on their experience from within the experiment.

To sum up – when testing a prototype within a performative framework: ensure the material situation has been carefully prepared; establish tasks and rules that are based on actions; observe/document the results and, accordingly, amend rules and repeat the experiment; and evaluate the prototype in terms of its performative effectiveness (Is this artefact conducive of the right kind of bodily actions? Is it appropriately responsive to bodies?).

PERCEPTUAL FRAMEWORK

Testing a prototype within a perceptual framework means that we are setting problems of a material or sensory nature, be it visual or sonic, tactile, olfactive, etc. These problems are usually related to an aesthetic or kinetic quality we are looking to achieve. If there are many possibilities to achieve such a quality, or if there are no definite ways of doing so, then prototyping is needed. For instance, when looking to create textured surfaces that evoke brittleness, we have a range of materials at our disposal, and different ways of using these materials will produce different types of crackled surfaces. How many materials can be considered? How many different types of cracks can be created? What are the different visual forms of brittleness achievable with a given material? Any sensory quality has a range or magnitude. If we explore this magnitude, we discover intricacies that shift the perceptual understanding of the artefact (which may or may not be appropriate).

Perceptual problems may also be elaborated specifically in relation to mimicry, whereby we are exploring how one material can emulate another: for instance, how wood may look like marble, or how the surface of canvas may appear like the surface of human skin. Problems of mimicry are essentially to do with deception, thus the perceptual conditions by which deception is achieved are likely to be as important as the physical treatment of a material made to emulate another. Canvas treated to appear like skin may only do so at a certain distance and under certain kinds of lighting.

Thus, when we are testing prototypes under a perceptual framework, much attention must be paid to the conditions within which we are working and observing the work: Which types of lighting enhance or inhibit the material qualities of the artefact (e.g. tungsten, halogen, LED or fluorescent lighting will have different impacts on the same artefact: highlighting or obscuring texture and colour, for instance)? What distances and viewpoints provide the most effective conditions to perceptually articulate the artefact? Taking note of these as part of the documentation of the tests will ensure that successful findings can be reflected upon and reproduced.

To sum up – when testing a prototype within a perceptual framework: define tasks based on modulating degrees of the perceptual qualities you are looking for; be aware and able to manipulate the environmental conditions under which you are testing your prototype; and evaluate by sensory observation and experience, and document your findings with precision.

RECORDING FINDINGS

Recording the findings made through prototyping is important for reflecting on, and analysing, the findings, as well as for capturing and replicating the logistics that made these findings possible.

Rehearsal by Christine Bach. This is a rehearsal of a mixed-media performance that includes props and video projection. The performer's use of props is timely, related to the pre-recorded content of projection. As such, the prototyping here is concerned with, and evaluated on, the basis of the precise correlation of bodily actions, props and video projection. JEMIMA YONG

Thus, documentation has creative and technical functions here. Creatively, documentation gives us more time to reflect on and evaluate prototypes: whilst we may perceive certain tests as successful or unsuccessful as they happen, our evaluation of these after they have happened may be very different. So we want to reflect as testing occurs, in a way that Donald Schön (1983) calls *reflection-in-action*, as well as reflect shortly and a while after testing (what Schön refers to as ad hoc and post hoc kinds of *reflection-on-action*). Documentation, then, is essential in facilitating a multifarious process of reflection that is likely to be more fruitful in identifying a lot more findings. Textual, drawn, photographic and video documentation should all be considered. And it is important that such documentation is undertaken through both objective and subjective lenses, i.e. as a matter of capturing as much of what happened, as well as what we have observed during the testing of prototypes. To do so, it is best to organize the tools for documenting in two ways: some of them should be positioned so as to record our viewpoint, and some should be positioned in a different and broader viewpoint. When using video cameras, for instance, one might be hand-held by ourselves and another might be attached to a tripod.

In addition to observing and documenting the creative results of prototyping, we must also attend to, and capture, the technical conditions by which these results are obtained. The technical aspect of this documentation is likely to be schematic, wherein simple drawings outline the material components at play in the tested prototype and are annotated with key data: for instance, dimensions, distances and angles. Ground plans can be helpful in documenting precise material and spatial information, crucial to replicate the work. But these do not capture the timely dimension of the experiment, which is crucial if the prototype is a timely event. Indeed, the movement of things during prototyping can be, to some extent, perceptually captured by video and technically recorded by schematics. However, these forms of documentation are primarily visual and, as such, may not grasp the full intricacies of the time factor.

This is often the case with performative prototyping where we are testing, for instance, the correlation of live physical actions with props and pre-recorded video projection and sound – we are testing the intersection of three types of phenomena. Some of these may only be partially visible on a camera, as hidden actions may be required on the part of the performer.

Thus, we need another form of documentation that will capture the precise timing of how different elements effectively intersect. This is what, in theatre, we call a cue list (*see* opposite). Cues are the markers of a trigger for a new action that may be done by the body or any other scenographic elements. As an example, let's describe a particular situation and convert it to a cue list: a video is projected on a wall, showing a film in which, at some point, a bird appears standing on a branch before flying off; a performer is sitting still and, as the bird appears on the projection, the performer reveals a feather, then, as the projected bird starts flying, the performer slowly brings the feather above their head and, as the bird disappears from the projection, the performer plants the feather into their hair. Here we have a simple performative action that is tightly aligned with a projection. To be able to replicate this situation, the performer will need to know how long each phase of the action must be: revealing the feather, bringing the feather over their head and planting it in their hair. Similarly, if the video projection needs to be operated by human hands, the operator will need to know the exact moment of the visual cue to turning the projection on and off.

When prototyping this situation we might very well try two kinds of cueing relations: one, where projection is triggered according to body movements and another where body movements are triggered by content in the projection. We shall further explore different speeds at which these actions can be performed. Revealing the feather could take a second or a minute. The video projection of the bird could appear just before, just

Cue List

Cue number	Cue description	Action	Timing of the action
1	Performer starts opening hand	Bird video fades in	5sec
2	Bird flies off the branch	Performer moves feather over head	10sec
3	Bird comes out of video frame	Performer plants feather in hair	0sec (simultaneous)

after or exactly at the same time as the feather is revealed. After trying out as many possibilities as possible, it is likely that one particular timely combination of these elements will be the most effective. Let's say that the following is the chosen best combination: the projection of the bird standing on a branch fades in to view as the performer opens their hand to reveal a feather in 5sec, at which point the projected bird starts flying off the branch and the performer moves the feather over their head in 10sec; in a snap moment, the performer plants the feather in their hair and the bird comes out of the video frame. The cue list for this situation is given in the table.

The cue list tells us that the movement of the performer will first dictate the operation of the projection. Subsequently, the performer's next action is triggered by the content of video projection. Finally, the performer's action and the video projection are exactly synchronized: in this case, the performer will need to count 10sec from the moment the bird flies off the branch before planting the feather in their hair. Cue lists can be helpful to capture and reproduce performative structures that are complex due to the timely intersection of various elements and media. As such, cue lists become essential to precisely render the practical composition of a performance over time, so that it can be run again and again with consistency. Final cue lists are precious documents for all those that are operating and running a performance. Performers memorize (through physical experience) the parts of these cue lists that concern them in the last phase of rehearsals, otherwise called run-throughs. Thus, cue lists are an important form of documentation to transition to, and eventually consolidate, the final composition of the work.

PROFESSIONAL INSIGHT

SITING
Sophie Jump

Sophie Jump designs for theatre and performance and won the overall Gold Medal at World Stage Design 2013. She is Co-Artistic Director and Designer for the performance company Seven Sisters Group, who are well known nationally and internationally for their site-specific work. Her designs were selected to represent the United Kingdom at every Prague Quadrennial exhibition of world theatre design between 1999 and 2011. She is a Linbury Prize for Stage Design committee member and was a judge for the 2015 Linbury Prize.

I have worked with the Seven Sisters Group to create productions in sites from the earliest days of my career. I became Associate Director of the company in 2006 and since then Artistic Director Susanne Thomas and I have developed the concepts for Seven Sisters Group shows together. Our work is almost exclusively site-specific and is always devised. Locations are sometimes the inspiration for the themes of a production or, at other times, we may come to a site with a theme that we want to explore in it. In either case, the place in which the performance happens has a massive impact on the creation of the work.

In this section I am going to be talking through my way of working when creating a piece of work in a site.

First Impressions
Susanne and I will visit the space together and our first encounter with it is important. We may be taken on a guided tour of the space or we may be allowed to wander at will but, in either case, it is vital to carefully observe the space and note our responses to it. The following are the main areas that we consider on our first site visit:

Architecture Is there anything unusual about the architecture? Is it grand, or domestic? Is it meant to make you feel intimidated or welcomed? Is it a leisure or work space? Is there a particular focus to the architecture (a church, for example, is arranged so that you look to one end and raise your eyes)? Is it a space that suggests a particular kind of behaviour?

Atmosphere How does the space make us feel? Is it spooky, exciting, curious, intimidating, overwhelming, etc.?

Social history of the space Has the space always been used for the same purpose? If not, are there traces of its former life? If it has always been the same, how might the users' behaviour have altered or stayed the same over the years?

Physicality of the users If the space is a public one, or is still in use, we will observe the way people behave in the space. How do they carry themselves? What are they doing? Are they relaxed or tense? Are they emotional or business-like?

Viewpoints What are good viewpoints for the audience in the space? Where could they be and where could the performers be placed to create interesting tensions? Looking across a large space perhaps, or in a more intimate proximity? Where could surprising things happen?

Personal responses We try not to edit our first responses and ideas, but rather to allow ourselves to react instinctively. What spaces or areas are we attracted to and why? What images and themes spring to mind? Does it suggest a film, a play or a book or a particular character? Are there themes that come to mind? We would not restrict our responses at this stage to what is achievable or realistic, but rather allow any ideas to surface.

This way of working changes very little if we come to a site with a theme we want to pursue. We are still responding to what we come across in the location but we might already be looking out for areas or viewpoints that could reflect or reinforce what we have in mind.

Research and Analysis
After visiting the space, I will go away and do a lot of research.

I will find images that seem to represent my response to the site. It is unlikely that I will find one image that says everything, so I find a lot of images that might each suggest something about

taken from walkway looking downwards

taken from walkway straight across

view backwards
down these stairs

Panorama: a collage of images created to give an idea of the different viewpoints in the atrium of the Ashmolean Museum (Oxford) for the Seven Sisters Group production of *Atalanta* (2010).

the responses and ideas that Susanne and I discussed at our first site visit.

I will also research into the site and its history. Perhaps looking for images or textual references to it, or finding out about similar locations; places that have, or had, similar uses and similar architecture.

I research the social history of the place. Finding, for example, paintings or photos of people using the space or similar kinds of spaces.

I will likewise research the themes that came to mind during the site visit. Perhaps locating myths, legends, plays, books, films or artworks that already deal with those themes.

Sifting

Susanne may also have done some visual research, or at least have further thoughts, and the next step is for us to meet and go through all the research material together. Conversations around this are really helpful for sifting through what seems useful, what we both still find exciting and interesting. An image that seemed significant to me might also trigger something in Susanne, and lead us to new places, or it might be cast aside as irrelevant. In this way we are refining ideas, finding the ones that we want to keep working on and perhaps triggering new ones.

(continued overleaf)

(continued from previous page)

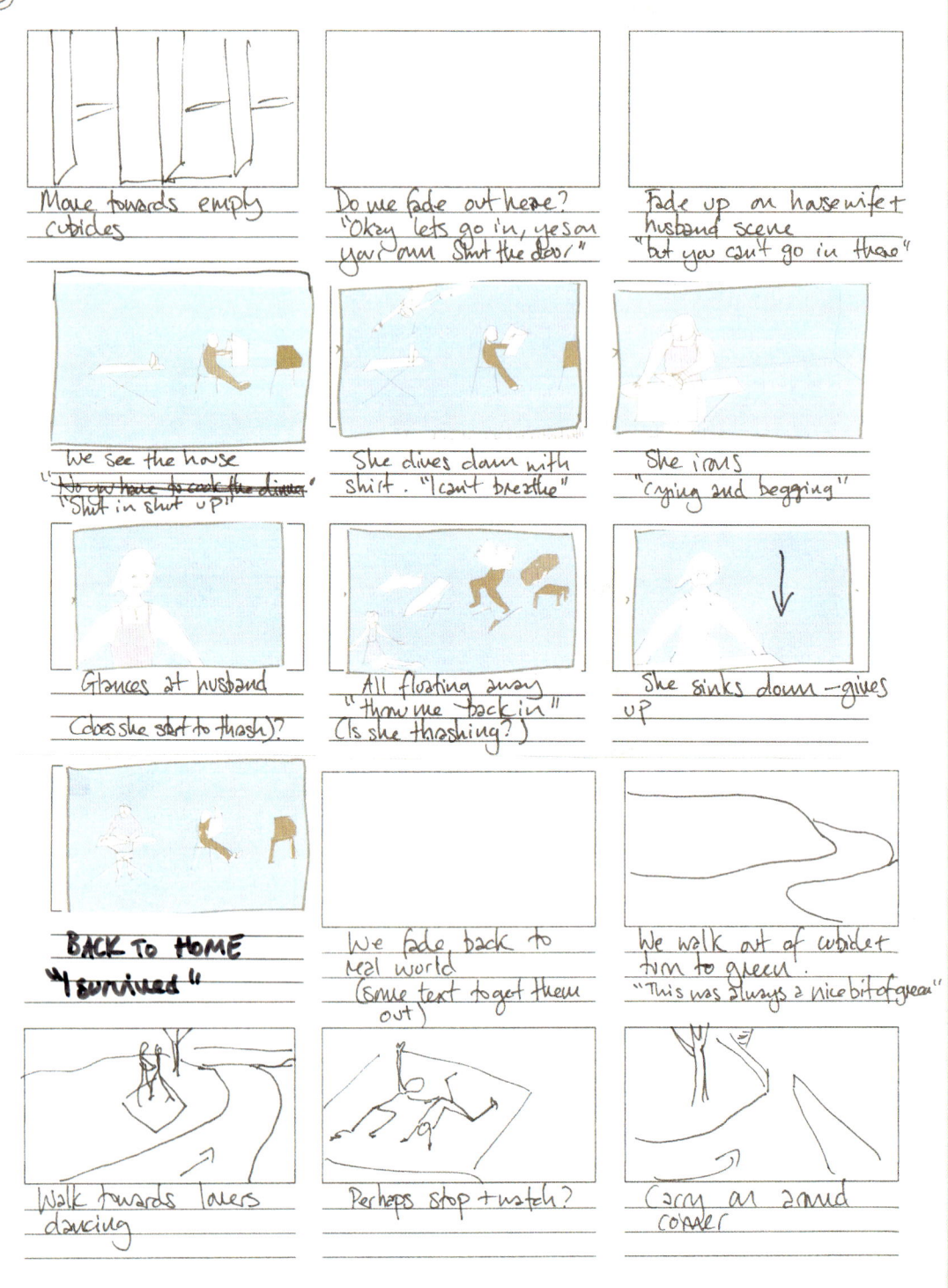

③

Move towards empty cubicles	Do we fade out here? "Okay lets go in, yes on your own. Shut the door"	Fade up on housewife + husband scene "but you can't go in there"
We see the house ~~Do you have to cook the dinner~~ "Shut in shut up"	She dives down with shirt. "I can't breathe"	She irons "crying and begging"
Glances at husband (does she start to thrash?)	All floating away "throw me back in" (Is she thrashing?)	She sinks down – gives up
BACK TO HOME "I survived"	We fade back to real world (some text to get them out)	We walk out of cubicle turn to green. "This was always a nice bit of green"
Walk towards lovers dancing	Perhaps stop + watch?	Carry on around corner

This meeting will probably lead to more research and there might be several sifting meetings before the next stage.

Working With Collaborators
Once we have a clear idea of the themes we want to work on, we will start to bring in collaborators, depending on what we feel we need. So, this could be a writer, initially, or we could get some performers together and start working physically in the space. We usually try to have a research period some weeks or months before we launch into the full production, so that we have time to further refine and develop the shape of the work and our ideas.

How the Process Differs from Working on a Text in a Theatre
There are certain tools and methods that have been created for the process of working on a text in a theatre space that are not relevant to devising work in a site, particularly if, as is almost always the case with Seven Sisters Group work, the audience is not static.

Traditionally, designs are planned before rehearsals even start and a model box presented at the first rehearsal as a way to share the proposals and to allow others to visualize them at full scale. A model does not seem necessary to Seven Sisters Group because we create the work in the space itself and I ensure that I am present at nearly every rehearsal so that I can directly input into the development of the piece and into the way the space is used. I rarely intervene in a site by bringing in structures, rather we are manipulating the space in subtle ways, e.g. the route or viewpoints of the audience and the placing of the performers, props or installations.

With large productions, however, I will create storyboards, plans and sketches to explain the route the audience will take and, in the case of our multimedia productions, how the real and digital will be layered. I will also often create a map of some kind for us to work from. This could be very rough and acts as an aide for discussions of what happens where, and planning the logistics of the audience and performer movements. Sometimes, however, it may be more useful to take a film of the route or photos of particular views we want to use and to combine them with sketches or drawings to explain our intentions.

Costumes
In the same way that, in a traditional process, a model box is produced before rehearsals start, the costumes are usually designed ahead of time. When working with Seven Sisters Group, however, because I am in nearly all the rehearsals, I have the opportunity to try costumes out as the piece develops. However, if the production is a large-scale or complicated one, then I may have to make decisions about costumes before we get started on creating the piece

In most cases I will keep bringing costumes along to try them out and see how they work with the space and the way that the performance is developing. Occasionally, I will have an image in mind quite early on of what colours or style the costumes could be, so I make them and bring them to rehearsals to test them out. There have also been productions when the costumes have only come together towards the end of the process, when I have a clearer picture of the piece as a whole.

Working in this responsive way means that the costumes sometimes feed into the movements or character development and, occasionally, if developed early enough, they can define the movement that is possible.

In conclusion, my main tips for working on devised performance in a site would be to ensure that you take careful note of your first reactions to, and thoughts about, the space. Second, to be involved in rehearsals as much as possible and to find ways to input your visual and spatial ideas into that process.

OPPOSITE: Storyboard: a working storyboard for the film that the audience followed on their iPods. It shows proposals for the layering of text, visuals and audience movement for the Seven Sisters Group production of *Like a Fish Out of Water* at Hillingdon and Hampton Lidos (2012).

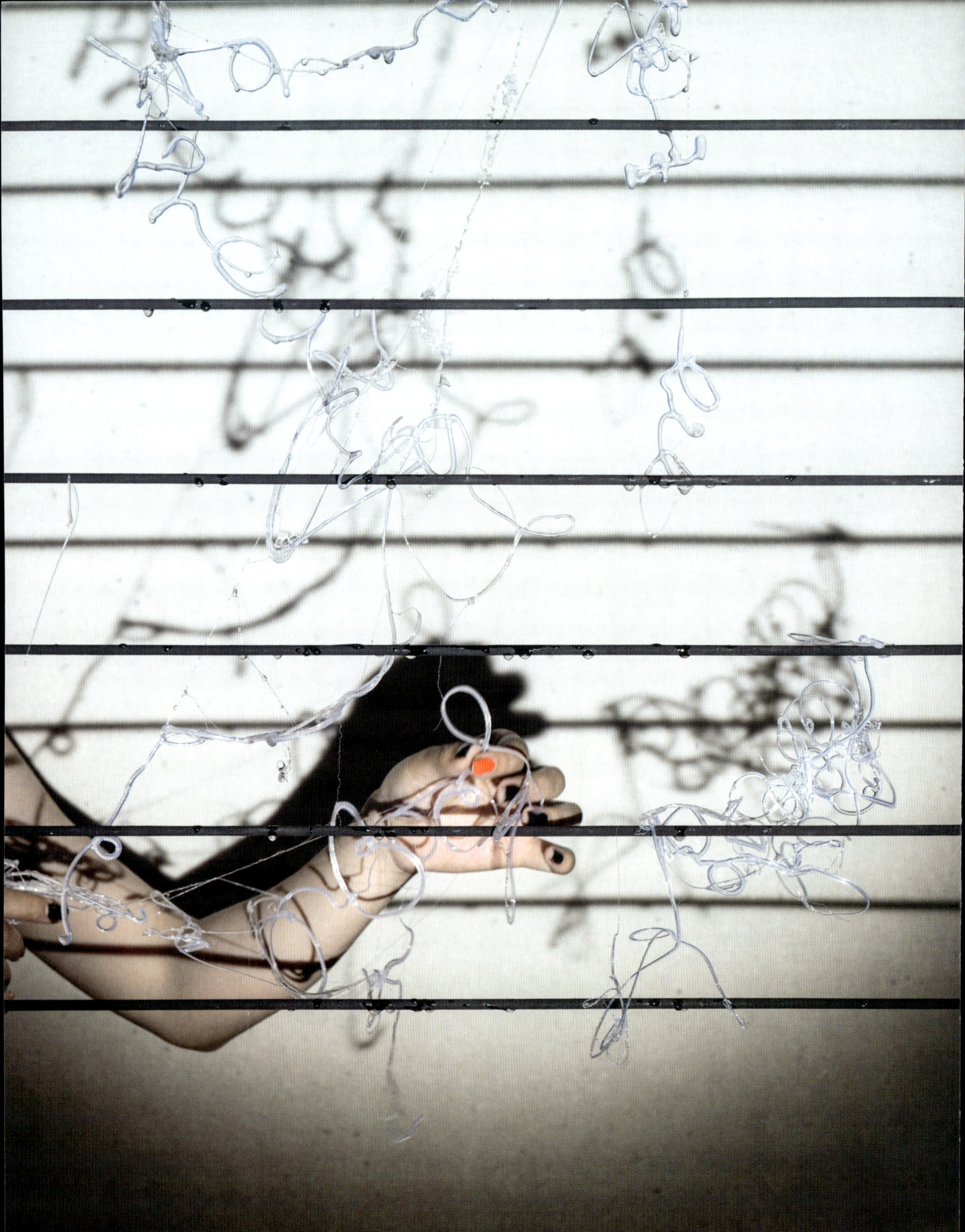

4
COMPOSING

Composition is the arrangement of various elements into one united structure. In music, a variety of notes, instruments and paces are correlated to form a single score. In dance, a variety of bodies, movements and rhythms are integrated together to create a choreography. In scenography, a variety of artefacts, phenomena and images are organized to establish what we might simply call an environment. Although sounds and bodies are often implicit in scenographic composition, they may very well be an explicit aspect, as we shall see. So we could say that scenographic composition is the scoring or choreographing of the environment.

Different eras and cultures have created different rules of composition, many of which are still found in today's practices. At the same time, in response to these rules, idiosyncratic tactics of composition have emerged and resulted in innovative models of structuring environments, bodies, sounds and so on. As with any creative practice, understanding how composition was and is achieved is very helpful in enabling us to develop our own ways. Indeed, some rules or strategies of composition might work better for some practitioners and less so for others. How we then alter, adapt and transform these will define how unique our compositional approach may be.

Although I have already touched on a range of compositional tools such as models, storyboards and prototypes, all of these have so far been discussed only in relation to creative conception and the development of a design. However, all these tools are also used to finalize composition in order to realize it. In other words, models, storyboards and prototypes are all crucial to develop and consolidate composition. In this chapter, I shall discuss the consolidation of composition, not by again addressing its tools but by discussing a range of compositional strategies that should be considered in practice. These are not rules *per se*, but rather modes that have inherent practical implications. I shall start with explaining the fundamentals of traditional, modernist and contemporary composition of forms, before moving on to elaborating on some key compositional facets in scenography, such as movement, colours and narration.

TRADITIONAL COMPOSITION

In the Renaissance, the composition of space and the environment (whether interior or exterior) was symbolically important, as it sought to represent human progress and intellect. Various rules based on mathematical and scientific discoveries, such as the Golden Ratio, were, therefore, at the heart of compositional practices (painting, architecture, urbanism, etc.). Human ideals of progress were reflected in constructed environments. The developments of the *camera obscura* and, subsequently, of linear perspective exemplify these ideals. Having discovered that human vision can be broken down into consistent mathematical units, if considered through only one human eye (monoscopic vision), visual and environmental compositions were designed through new perspectival rules:

OPPOSITE: *Unwriting* by Lingge Ma. PATRICK BALDWIN

Scale model by Anca Niculescu depicting set design for Pedro Calderon de la Barca's *Life is a Dream* (1635). Note how the set denotes traditional composition by way of symmetry, highlighting the vantage point at the centre, and closing down, or containing, the stage to conceal its backstage areas: turning the stage into a window on another world.

foreground, midground and background were now arranged according to a unique (one-eyed) vantage point.

Linear perspective served as a compositional rule to conceive of, and construct, a perfected vision of our environment. Monoscopic vision stabilizes the messiness of stereoscopy (two-eyed vision). As you know, when looking at your environment with one eye and then with the other, your perception of positions and distances will shift. To reconcile these discrepancies between what each eye is seeing, the brain makes adjustments, convergences and fills gaps. But although the brain does manage to reconcile the visions from the left and the right eye, it does not fix/stabilize what we see as well as if only one eye is open. Stereoscopic vision (two-eyed vision, or the way most of us actually see) was thus deemed less reliable. Within this same tradition, the frame becomes paramount to further stabilizing vision. Just as wooden frames were necessary to mathematically define one-eyed vision in the early experiments of *camera obscura*, the proscenium arch would thus become the conditional frame of theatrical composition. First, the frame provides axial references according to which the vantage point is defined and, thus, all other elements are arranged. Second, the frame forces the viewer to engage in frontal vision by neatly delineating the otherwise blurred boundary between frontal and peripheral vision. This is important because the periphery of the visual field remains fuzzy, even in one-eyed vision.

Thus, a traditional approach to composition involves:

- An underlying symmetry ruled by the vantage point.
- A clear layering of, and thus distinction between, foreground, midground and background.
- A frontal perception that gives the illusion that the frame actually contains the world on stage by way of emphasizing the visual borders around it.
- Clarity and stability of the relation between figure and the background against which it is perceived.
- Providing a homogenic view of the stage shared by all audiences.

MODERNIST COMPOSITION

The second approach to composition worth generalizing here then is modernism. Somewhere located between the middle of the nineteenth century and early twentieth century, modernism was infused by artistic movements considered as avant-garde. Simply put, their innovation revolved

Scale model by Fiona Martin depicting a site-specific scenic design for a dance performance. The design is reminiscent of modernist composition, as it is referencing the symmetry of traditional composition whilst, at the same time, preventing spatial clarity: foreground and background are merged into a single yet fragmented environment where borders and limits are unclear.

around the deconstruction of traditional composition: for instance, the perspectival arrangement of three-dimensionality was dismantled by cubist artists by getting rid of the vantage point (which is a singular viewpoint) and instead using multiple viewpoints to explode the object of perception accordingly; the continuity of positive spaces (subtly punctuated by negative spaces) was reversed by Impressionist artists who emphasized visual gaps to produce discontinuous and fleeting images. As the representation of three-dimensionality is broken, complicated and distorted, the image hovers between three-dimensionality and two-dimensionality, and the viewer is required to engage more actively in decoding the image.

Compositional abstraction thus arises in modernism as a way to challenge the traditional conventions of composition. A modernist approach then references and subverts traditional composition by exploring:

- Heterogenic views (perception of the image differ from one point of view to another).
- Unfixed/shifting borders resulting in the discontinuity and ambiguity of foreground, midground and background.
- Perceptual imbrication of two-dimensionality and three-dimensionality.

In Dallas Wexler's speculative design for Maurice Ravel's *L'Enfant et les Sortileges* (1925), multiple moving frames with screens are arranged in a way that delineates the three axes that determine the traditional Cartesian coordinate system of three-dimensional space (x, y, z): the edges of the screen on the floor provide clear demarcations of the width and depth of the set, whilst the edges of

Digital model for *L'Enfant et les Sortileges* (1925) by Dallas Wexler. The design is in line with modernist composition, as it fulfils the symmetry of traditional composition whilst refusing to contain the stage and conceal its backstage: this is evidently done by way of leaving large, empty areas on stage around the scenic structure, thereby seemingly bringing the offstage to exposure on stage.

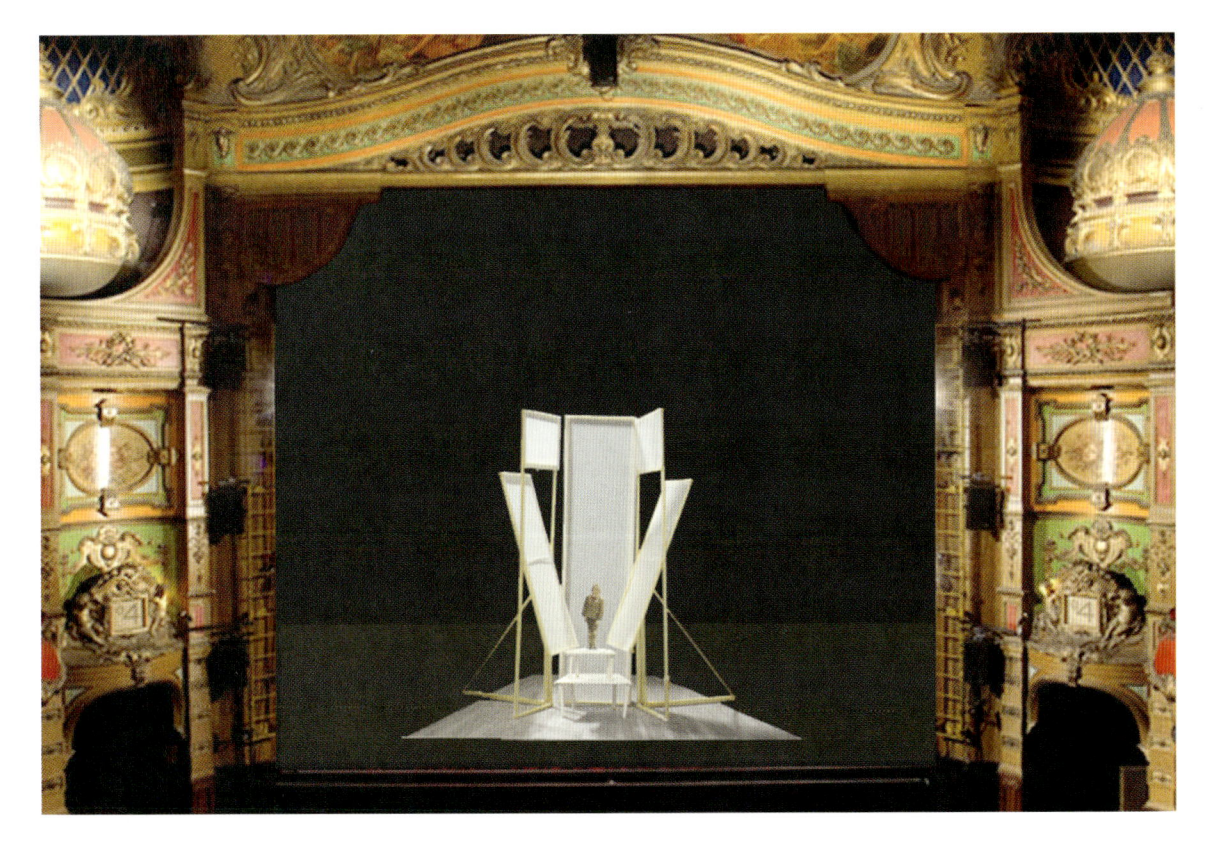

Digital model for *L'Enfant et les Sortileges* (1925) by Dallas Wexler. This scenic design is made of frames that echo the overall stage frame of the proscenium arch, yet the multiple frames move, opening and closing, to produce a rather abstract space merging three-dimensionality and two-dimensionality – another key aspect of modernist composition.

the vertical frames form the vertical axis. All three axes intersect at the vantage point located at the very centre of the stage to produce a perfectly symmetrical structure, as warranted by traditional composition. Aligned with this tradition, the protagonist (here the Child) is located at the centre, right above the vantage point.

However, this scenic structure also deviates from, and subverts, traditional composition: although the set parallels the frame of the proscenium arch, it is not flush with it. This creates an explicit gap between the set and the frame of the proscenium arch resulting in an overall scenic structure that seems to be partly floating in space. This is a subversion of another important aspect of traditional composition, which is the use of negative space or the unoccupied space between things. Traditionally, the negative space is implicit as it serves the purpose of articulating that which must be seen (performers, their movements and interactions): in this sense, the negative has the syntactic function of discretely punctuating that which is visible. Here, this traditional function of the negative space is augmented, highly visible and almost caricatured.

The modernist twists on traditional composition are particularly blatant then in terms of:

- The multiplication of the proscenium into multiple frames creates a redoubling of containment (the scenic space delineates a container within a container), which exposes and ignores the theatrical container. Although, the symmetry of the frames produces a traditional equilibrium, their slight separations create a modernist discontinuity.

- The quantity of two-dimensional surfaces (screens) dominates over the physically three-dimensional and bordered environment of the stage, yet together the screens suggest another three-dimensional space that is open to its surrounding. As the screens move, they modulate this scenic openness and its incomplete three-dimensionality.

CONTEMPORARY COMPOSITION

Modernism has made a lasting mark on composition ever since its inception in the early twentieth century. Many key compositional qualities of modernist works have continued evolving in some cases still with respect to traditional composition and in other cases moving further away from the tradition. These latter cases have sometimes been qualified under the term postmodernism as they appeared to move away from modernism itself. Yet the term postmodernism has come to be defined in a variety of (sometimes conflicting) ways so, for the purpose of addressing the next and most recent phase in composition, I shall refer to it as simply contemporary composition. Needless to say that contemporary composition, strictly speaking, is any form of composition currently undertaken that includes an array of traditional, modernist and postmodernist strategies. In this section, however, contemporary composition will only be used with regard to current strategies that have moved beyond traditional and modernist conventions.

Modernism demonstrated that the breaking of traditional rules of composition resulted in the productive development of modes of perception not based on an ideal monoscopic/perspectival vision of the world but on the more messy, stereoscopic, moving and variable vision of the body. Whereas traditional composition sought to control the eye of the observer, modernist composition destabilized this control to instigate more autonomy and freedom in the observer in the act of perceiving. Not based on mathematical or geometric ideals, but on the material reality of the body, modernist composition opened the door to reconsidering composition on the basis of natural phenomena (rather than man-made intellectual constructs). Contemporary strategies of composition that have moved further away from tradition using the new avenues opened by modernism, have done so by ways of generating compositions out of random and self-organizing principles that are perceivable in the natural world: aleatoric growth of organisms and plants, movement and spacing of rain drops and animal groups and so on. Jackson Pollock's *Action Painting* exemplifies the contemporary attempt at creating a composition that somehow composes itself. Evidently, there is still a certain level of control here, but the effort is placed on enabling chance-based composition. Randomness may be achieved through accidental and unpredictable procedures, material conditions of composition that weaken our control. In these kinds of procedures, repetition is a determinant factor. For instance, tearing a sketch into smaller pieces and mixing these up rapidly to form a new image can produce an endless amount of new images, some of which will be more surprising than others (surprising because it is so different from the original image that was torn apart). Thus, it is worth repeating the procedure many times. Any resulting image will be fragmented to some extent. But some kind of cohesion may emerge from the fragmentation, whereby different parts are separated yet connected. We could call this apparently paradoxical quality of contemporary composition a branching. Indeed, as it happens with trees, we perceive leaves, branches, trunks and roots as connected yet differing elements, as green smooth oval leaves grow out of brown rough linear branches. Branching involves a continuous and dynamic connection of disparate components: movement is, therefore, an implicit or explicit aspect of branching. When we are dealing with images of broken artefacts, for instance, branching is what keeps the different fragments cohesive. What does a broken tiled floor look like? We all have an answer/image for this, and we can render it. But

Scale model by Dina Salem Levy depicting a set design for Arnold Schoenberg's *Pierrot Lunaire* (1912). This labyrinth of mirrored walls complicates the perception of the three-dimensional space in such a way that there is no longer a structure of foreground/midground/background. Although there are multiple walls, each area of the set is visually borderless. The eyes of the viewer can never settle on a focal point but have to constantly shift their focus: an asset of contemporary composition.

the branching (the cohesive connectedness) of the different ceramic fragments can be variable, depending on what caused the floor to break. A tiled floor will break very differently if a heavy object has fallen on it or if an earthquake has taken place. The gaps and crevices between the different fragments will implicitly tell a story that is the cohesive thread that connects the various fragments. There are always multiple ways of branching, multiple ways of ordering within the apparent chaos.

A contemporary approach to composition is then concerned with:

- Unframing: multiple and overlapping frames that prevent framing itself result in the loss of linear perspective, of the vantage point and of a central point of focus, instead producing an all-encompassing periphery that offers multiple and changing viewpoints.
- Three-dimensional complexity within which the body has a dynamic and unfixed sets of positions in space
- Branching: transformation through repetition.

Scale model by Kristina Petrova for *A Dream Play* (Caryl Churchill's 2005 adaptation of August Stringberg's 1901 play). The scenic space is made of fragments of areas imbricated into one another so as to form an island that has door frames but neither walls nor doors. This creates a space that is at once singular and multiple, interior and exterior, without a centre or a periphery: these are some of the characteristics of contemporary composition.

In Kristina Petrova's speculative stage design for *A Dream Play* (Caryl Churchill's 2005 version of August Stringberg's 1901 play), the scenic environment comprises of various areas in which walls are missing. The areas then are implied by various levels and frames that fuse into one overall jigsaw puzzle that forms a circular island revolving on itself. Where a room ends and another starts is visually unclear due to how the rooms have been physically imbricated and woven into one another, and due to the constant pivoting movement of the overall structure. As a result, the foreground keeps becoming the background and returning to the fore. Depending on their locations, viewers will perceive differing spatial arrangements.

Furthermore, the open frames and borders of the set suggest that every point in space is an entrance and an exit: in other words, there is no inside and outside. And although the circularity of scenery necessarily involves a centre point and a periphery (evident if we take a bird's-eye view on the set), the frontal view of this scenic structure reveals a varying range of material levels (or heights), which obscures the understanding of a centre to augment the periphery. Somehow kaleidoscopic then, the composition of this design relies on movement and rhythm: on one hand there is the continuous and monotonous movement of the revolving set and everything standing on it, and on the other hand, there is the discontinuous

Scale model in motion by Kristina Petrova for *A Dream Play* (Caryl Churchill's 2005 adaptation of August Stringberg's 1901 play). This scenic design also proposes to make use of a revolving stage so that its whole scenery constantly and slowly revolves on itself. As such, the audience can see every scenic area in turns but can never perceive the entire scenic environment at once.

and sporadic movement of bodies stepping up and down the various scenic levels to navigate the set. No visual element on stage is fixed, everything moves at various paces. As such, composition becomes more a case of animation than depiction. And whenever kinesis drives forms, we must ask ourselves a range of compositional questions to do with the dynamics of speed and rhythm.

MOVEMENT IN COMPOSITION

When dealing with movement, we are dealing with trajectories, with the way something emerges, evolves and comes to an end. Moreover, it is often the case that the emergence of something overlaps with the end of something else: then we are dealing with two movement trajectories superimposed at some point. In the fields of dance and music, concerns with speed and rhythm have led to various taxonomies of kinetic qualities that are very helpful for us to be aware, and make use, of the full range of options.

Here I shall use Laban's *Eight Basic Efforts* to unpack the palette of movements in our hands. Following Laban, we can first break movement down to three basic qualities: strength, speed and direction. However, each of these qualities is, in fact, a spectrum of movement dynamics. Each kinetic spectrum then can be further broken down

Exercises For Rendering Movement

Rendering the kinetic qualities of a moving object can be a challenge. As Laban did, we can use words to describe these qualities. But whenever the object in motion is not one we would expect to see moving, it can be difficult to imagine how it might move in a particular way. Therefore, we have to have ways of making movement as suggestively clear as possible. The following task aims at supporting you in developing your own approach. For each of Laban's eight movement qualities described in the text above, you are going to draw two kinds of illustrative sketches.

1. The first kind is purely schematic: draw up the outlines of a cube for each Laban movement quality (punching, dabbing and gliding, for example) and inside each cube represent the movement quality by drawing only lines and arrows. Lines can be straight or curved, continuous or broken, thick or thin. Arrows can be short or elongated, wide-angled, narrow-angled or right-angled, thick or thin. Since you are illustrating the movement qualities in a cube, you can choose an invisible axis (always the same) within the cube on which to draw up your schematic representation of the movement qualities. When you are finished with each of Laban's effort qualities, compare them; if some of them look quite similar, go back to them and alter them so as to become more distinct. Do all those lines and arrows clearly communicate different movements to you? If so, then you may now have a system of notation for movement.

2. Another way of representing movement on a two-dimensional surface is found in the depiction of an object's various positions taken by way of moving on a singular surface, as if this object had left shadows or traces of its presence behind. The more complex the object, the more complicated this approach can get. So, to train yourself in obtaining a basic understanding of this kind of rendering, it is best to start with a simple object. For instance, take a handful of spaghetti (cooked and uncooked) and place them on a sheet of paper. Draw following the edges of each piece of spaghetti, this will evidently produce an array of lines. Now, to draw up the traces of the spaghetti moving according to Laban's effort qualities, you may either manipulate the spaghetti physically on paper and draw again around their edges, or you may remove the spaghetti from the paper and draw the trajectories between their traces. Is this messier approach more evocative of movement than the previous schematic approach? Or can you find a compromise between the two methods and which may produce a more explicit rendering of motion?

to its two opposite poles (between which exists a wide range of possibilities):

- Strength determines the weight of the movement: from strong movements (heavy, harsh and bold) to light movement (soft, gentle and discrete).
- Speed determines the rhythm of the movement: from sudden movements (distinct accelerations/decelerations) to sustained movements (gradual).
- Direction determines the axis of the movement: from direct movements (unilateral) to indirect movements (multilateral and flexible).

Strength that is exerted in some direction(s) and at some speed is movement. Laban further suggested a list of eight core movement dynamics, which are combinations of different types of strength, speed and direction.

Directional:

- Punching comprises of abrupt and forceful movements, such as the movement of the needle of a sewing machine piercing through fabric.
- Dabbing comprises of sudden and light movements, such as blowing a hair off your shoulder.

- Gliding comprises of sustained and soft movements, such as the gentle caress of a new-born baby.
- Pressing comprises of continuous and strong movement, such as shoving a heavy furniture down a corridor.

Indirect/multidirectional/flexible:

- Wringing comprises of sustained and strong movements, such as juicing a lime on a lemon squeezer.
- Floating comprises of continuous and soft movements, such as snowflakes meandering through a gentle breeze.
- Flicking comprises of sudden and light movements, such as a horse's tail striking flies off its croup.
- Slashing comprises of abrupt and forceful movements, such as speed skating on a fresh new sheet of ice.

We should also add one more type of movement:

- Still: stillness is largely considered to be the absence of movement, as it implies the lack of mobility. Yet, it may still be a type of movement that is barely perceivable or simply too slow to be grasped by the human eye; we could call it muted movement. Furthermore, the fact that something is not travelling in space does not necessarily mean that no movement is present. A human body, for instance, cannot be completely still. In stillness, movement dynamics are likely to be minute but they can still be a kind of punching (e.g. hiccupping) or floating (e.g. shivering).

COLOUR

As with materials, colours are far more complex than the mere words we use for them. To speak of the colour red helps define a range of existing colours but it does not point at one particular colour. To speak of the colour blood red refines this range further but it is still insufficient: the blood red of 1970s' Britain differs from that of 1920s' Germany. Language has continually been trying to capture the specificity of colours but colours constantly evolve. This is due to developments in the technical means used to create colours. Whilst we used to create colours out of natural pigments and binding agents, historical developments of colour-making show an ever-increasing use of complex chemical processes and man-made materials. Nowadays, nanotechnologies continue to provide us with new colour variations and vibrancies, such as a black darker than any other black.

So there are limitations in the way words can communicate colours. Thus, when working with colours, having material samples of colours is essential. Material samples are more precise than digital samples (on screens) because digital media change colours not only because they have their own colour settings, but also because they are light-based and thus operate on a different colour wheel than the physical colour wheel. Colours in all lighting, all TV and all digital media are based on the RGB additive colour model, wherein the primary colours are red, green and blue and the secondary colours are cyan, magenta and yellow. In this model, mixing green and red produces yellow. Rather differently, physical colours are based on the RYB or CMYK subtractive colour models, wherein the primary colours are red, yellow and blue, or cyan, magenta and yellow (the secondary colours in RGB model), with the secondary colours being purple, orange and green or red, blue and green. CMYK is the colour model used in printing processes. RYB concerns every other use of physical colours.

The visual perception of colours is a complex domain where general rules can be found but, given that no two bodies have exactly the same eyes, these rules should only be lightly considered. Nonetheless, there are two rules worth knowing, even though, again, there are some exceptions to these rules.

First, colours produce illusions of depth otherwise known as stereoptic depth perception or

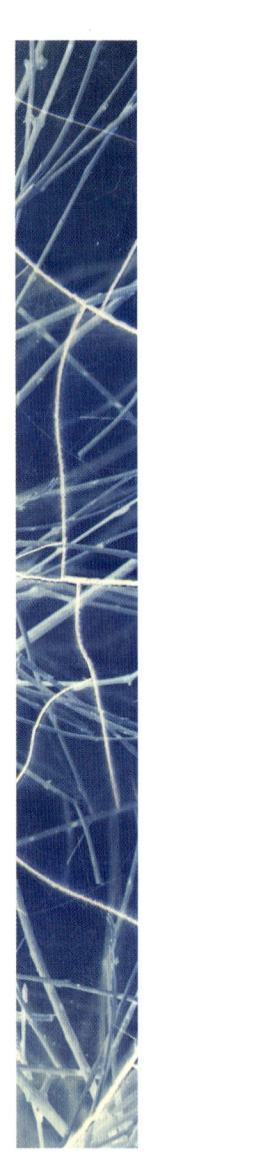

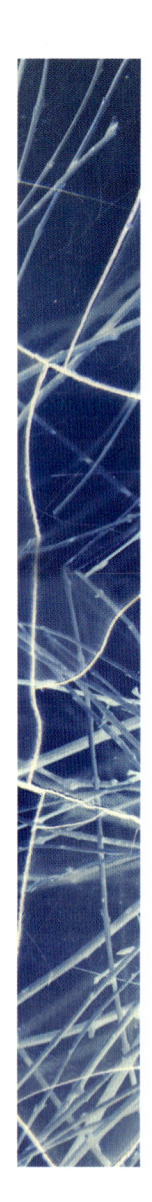

Variations on colour composition by Rita Torrao. Various types of the colour blue are considered to produce patterns of variable contrasts.

chromostereopsis: cold colours, especially blues, are receding (they give an illusion of distance and depth) and warm colours, especially reds, are advancing (they give an illusion of proximity and closeness). This is particularly explicit when these colours are placed right next to one another, which, in so doing, creates a rather conflicting, if not irritating, visual experience for the viewer. However, chromostereopsis is a helpful phenomenon to employ whenever we are looking to create a sense of depth or proximity with two-dimensional surfaces or to enhance depth within a three-dimensional set-up (painting the foreground components red and the background components blue will augment the overall depth of the space). Similarly, red may be considered whenever we are looking to highlight a detail as if placing a magnifying lens on it.

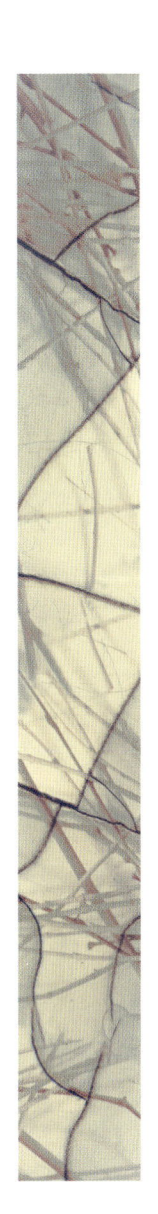

Second, the juxtaposition of colours in space (adjacently) or in time (consecutively) produces contrasting effects, which may change our perception of the colours. Simultaneous contrast is a phenomenon where the colours of two different and adjacent objects affect each other. This is particularly the case with complementary colours (i.e. colours located on the opposite ends of the colour wheel): if a red object is positioned right next to a blue object, red and blue may no longer appear as such, especially on the adjacent edges of these objects. In other words, unwanted colours and hues may start emerging as a result of the interaction of these colours in perception. Successive contrast is a phenomenon where the perception of a colour is affected by another colour that has just been seen. We may want to show a blue circle immediately following a red circle at the exact same spatial location but the red circle may not appear red as the perception of the colour blue remains, overlaps and affects the red. Furthermore, the juxtaposition of intense colours with light colours can modify the perception of these latter colours: the visually dominant, most intense, colour may affect the lighter one.

All these potential problems linked to colours tell us that imagery moving in time and space should not be composed as separate and fixed tableaux, otherwise successive contrast can generate colour disturbances that will unexpectedly modify the composition.

A change of colour is a change in sensation, emotion and meaning. Whilst we may all agree on that statement, to what extent can we control and compose with the emotional and symbolic values of colours? We are all surrounded by colours imbued with symbolism: in signage and traffic lights, in flags and emblems, in advertising and apps and so on. Colours have long been used for the purpose of communication. By way of constant exposure and habits, the symbolic function of colours is engraved in our psyche. Yet these are not universal but rather based on socio-cultural contexts. Beyond the symbolic value of the colour red in road signage, which is ubiquitous around the world, red has further symbolic values that differ across countries and cultures. These values are disparate because they have more profound social and cultural meaning and functions: the colour red in traffic signage communicates a simple message of prohibition; but in a flag or a political party's logo, colours stand for quasi-philosophical notions such as freedom or sovereignty. These are far more complex symbols and, indeed, the very notions of freedom or sovereignty do change over time, as well as take on very distinct definitions across cultures.

The symbolic function of colours then is not simply expedient with simple messages and injunctions related to law and order, as it is simultaneously imbued with philosophical and ideological values. A simplistic approach to colour symbolism can, therefore, run the risk of being misunderstood. This does not mean that we should not use colours but it does require us to be precise with colours and their hues. This is even more critical when juxtaposing colours since the associations of certain colours can resonate more clearly with very specific symbolism. For example, we might want to juxtapose the colours red and blue in order to create contrast and depth, but the particular shades of red and blue we might consider could inappropriately evoke a flag of sorts.

CONTRAST

Contrast creates dynamic tension in composition. Indeed, contrast is what allows something to be distinct from something else and, as such, to be perceived. Although the lack of contrast can be a compositional strategy, most often contrasts are required to highlight one or more elements within an overall composition. The juxtaposition of differing colours, textures, shapes and movements can create contrast: the greater their differences, the stronger the contrast. More structural and somehow discrete compositional assets can also produce contrast. For instance, introducing asymmetric elements in an otherwise highly symmetric image will inject a dynamic tension within the overall composition.

Negative spaces are another type of structural device for creating contrast. These are the spaces in-between things: the gaps that puncture and punctuate that which is visible. Negative spaces are a kind of punctuation because they articulate relations between components and thus hold the overall composition. Going back to the body, we can perceive hands because of the thin gaps or empty trenches found between the fingers. Although negative spaces are not necessarily meant to be perceived, they significantly support our perception of the composition. Furthermore, they create distance between things which, in turn, helps communicating the quality of their relations.

The negative space can also take centre stage and be a predominant feature of a composition. Renaissance painters like Caravaggio and

Scale model for Benjamin Britten's *The Turn of the Screw* (1954) by Minglu Wang. When symmetry is used as an overall design scheme, integrating asymmetric details creates a dynamic tension.

Rembrandt used the so-called technique of *chiaroscuro* to explore extreme contrasts by inserting bright elements surrounded by lots of darkness, albeit negative space. As mentioned before in relation to colours, contrast can create depth. In *chiaroscuro*, the predominance of dark negative spaces is perceptually receding, whilst the bright elements are advancing. The depth created by this juxtaposition is uncertain and unspecific but it provides the bright elements with a sense of three-dimensionality by way of visually dissolving into their surroundings.

The composition of negative spaces then is critical in the creation of depth and three-dimensionality. This does not solely concern designing empty pockets of space as spatial components themselves can act as negative spaces. In this way, the negative space starts producing meaning. In

Scale model for Georg Kaiser's *From Morning to Midnight* (1912) by Harriet Hickman. Dynamic contrasts can be created by including negative spaces that, here, are produced out of the material presence of black scaffolded structures.

Rembrandt's paintings, the heavy presence of the negative space of darkness is simply suggestive of nighttime. On the other hand, giving a physical presence and materiality to negative spaces can suggest various atmospheres of fragmentation, disorder and destruction.

Negative spaces are not solely dark and shaded areas: they may also be achieved through blur/fuzziness, as well as through achromatic colours (extremely light colours on the edge of neutrality, such as a hint of yellow or blue perceived in what might be referred to as an off-white colour). In these cases, the negative space creates a dissolve that may be less conspicuous but still allows for a gentle tension between components.

VISUAL NARRATIVE

We compose artefacts and environments to be used by bodies. These artefacts and environments may communicate meaning in themselves, yet it is the body's relation to, and interaction with, them that will effectively produce and clarify meaning. Now, communicating with words offers a degree of precision that facilitates the viewer's understanding of a narrative. On the other hand, perceptual communication can be more evasive. In performance, the structuring of meaning is called dramaturgy. A script is a textual system of narration that is recontextualized into time-based actions. Whilst words from the script are preserved in the form of speech, other words (typically stage directions) take on a perceptual form. Although both processes contribute to creating a dramaturgical understanding, the latter procedure of translating words into images is clearly scenographic and provides a different form of communication that I shall refer to as visual dramaturgy. Indeed, unlike the way words are primarily understood intellectually, images are first experienced in terms of sensations that are then decoded by intellectual means. Visual dramaturgy is thus a less direct form of communicating a narrative. These two forms of communication, though often woven together, take on further meaning in the way that they echo or relate to everyday communication and narratives.

In everyday life, we are regularly faced with images that have a clear and fixed meaning: road signs, for instance, constitute a form of codified imagery of a symbolic order. Symbols, indeed, are visual motifs constructed to communicate meaning. Everyday life is punctuated by symbols whose meaning is learnt and recorded through their various iterations. Thus, repetition is needed to consolidate the meaning of a visual motif. This is important to us if we are interested in creating new and meaningful visual motifs or if we are keen to give new meaning to an already existing visual motif. Indeed, a visual element that may not be fully understood in its first iteration, might become clearer as it becomes used again in different situations. In other words, it is through the iterative exposure of a motif that meaning is structurally produced over a given period of time. In turn, the repetition of a visual motif will produce a rhythm that has an impact on the meaning that is produced.

In theatre, we can see the opening and closing of the curtain, or the black-out on stage, as fundamental visual signals that produce a potent meaning: the beginning and the end of a story or an event. This meaning is so engrained that we do

Marketing photograph for JustAMust's production of *SportsPlay*; art direction by the author. The repetition and juxtaposition of multiple artefacts originating from different contexts can push these artefacts to communicate new meaning: here the co-existence of bathroom- and kitchen-related artefacts hints at the preparation and consumption of the human body.
LUDOVIC DES COGNETS

not need to process it intellectually, rather it triggers an immediate physical response: a silence, a gasp or applause. The repetition of a visual element thus conditions both the viewer's understanding and mode of being. Conversely, the breaking of learnt patterns places the viewer in a different situation. For instance, if the curtains fall down and yet something starts happening on stage (in front or behind the curtain), this conditioning is broken and the viewer becomes alert to the possibility of a new meaning. Because a known symbol and pattern is disrupted, its meaning is in question. Whereas the undisrupted use of this symbol had produced a kind of release in the viewer who finds herself in the comfort of a known meaning and behaviour, the disruption of that symbol will create a tension between image and viewer. What does this mean? What is going to happen next? How am I supposed to react? This tension is a more intense engagement that must be managed carefully. Indeed, as we upset the pre-existing knowledge of our audience, we are also taking the risk of disengaging them altogether. Therefore, there must be a suggestion that a new meaning is at play. This new meaning might be delivered all at once or gradually disclosed through the variable iteration of a new pattern.

Existing objects brought together from different contexts can generate new, meaningful associations. A particular object can be used according to another artefact or located in the place of a different type of object. This will cause what we may call a displacement of the object's usual context and its contextual value or meaning. For instance, artefacts like towels and bathrobes are meaningfully correlated with bathrooms and, more specifically, the grooming and cleansing of the body. If we relocate such artefacts in a kitchen and place them in active relations to kitchen utensils, we can start shifting their meaning from grooming/cleansing the body to cooking/consuming the body. This new meaning can be further consolidated by way of repeating these artefacts so that they become a pattern. Furthermore, by mediating the active relation between artefacts and environment, the body here allows a kind of narrative to emerge: the grooming/cleansing of human flesh (typically conceived as a self-preserving action) is now perceived as a dangerous and absurd action on the edge of self-harm. This meaning raises questions as to the origin of this paradox (what happened for this shift to take place?) and the extent to which the body will go in this respect (will it consume itself?).

PROFESSIONAL INSIGHT

SPECTATING
Michael Pavelka

Michael Pavelka is a set and costume designer for the stage. He has designed for the RSC, National Theatre, UK and Irish regional theatres and many West End productions. His international work includes all the global touring productions of the Propeller Theatre Company along with other shows across North America, Africa and the Far East. He is currently Head of Design for Rutgers Conservatory at Shakespeare's Globe. He is author of So You want to Be a Theatre Designer? (2015).

Being, Seen: Questions on the Enigmatic Relationship Between You and Your Audience
The audience, your audience – who are they and what do they need from you? As artists and designers, can we, and should we, picture them clearly? In recalling Peter Brook's seminal definition of theatre as 'a man walks across this empty space whilst someone else is watching him' (Brook 1968: 9), practitioners are more likely to be preoccupied with the existential nature of the [wo]man, rehearse the walk and then tie themselves in knots about what 'empty' means, rather than the conditions of the watcher. Whether we have complete, or at least partial, control of the audience's situation – or whether we are powerless and at the mercy of box office pressures or a monolithic monster of architecture – to what extent should we position and frame the work with its audience in mind?

There is no doubt that the sensorial and sensual aspects of scenography, particularly the actions and images that are central to any artists' work, linger longer in the memory of the audience than what they meant at the time. The viewer usually needs afterthought to process the experience into an embedded concept.

The author caught on camera watching *The Mysteries* at the National Theatre in 1985. I actually, along with many others as you can see here, thought it was exceptional! Modified screenshot from www.youtube.com.

(continued overleaf)

(*continued from previous page*)

In anticipating your audience's arrival, you will be making conscious and subconscious assumptions about them, and buried not far beneath the surface of either, lurks the very real dangers of patronizing your patrons. But anticipate you must – acting out your expectations is at the core of your process. Without an audience, your work will be meaningless.

Not all the following questions are relevant to the circumstances of every work and context, but sometimes, the more oblique your self-questioning is, surprising and strangely powerful options can present themselves to you and your creative team. You may, as an artist, choose to only be true to the piece in hand, uncluttered by the distraction of double-guessing who will see it. However, it is more prudent to have asked the questions and dismissed them than not to have asked them at all. They were not conceived in any particular order but to lend it a narrative, each section is strung together in a sequence that you may confront them. You will, of course, dismiss some, find a better way of asking others and have plenty of your own.

Proximity
How far have your audience travelled to see the work? How will their journey 'colour' their experience of it? For example, how does the local climate impact on the work?
Do you want your audience to have a single or multiple experiences?
Is the audience aware of the shape of (a) the space(s) they occupy? and (b) the whole space? Will they be seeing your work as a collective, as a group of collectives or as a group of individuals?
What are the dimensional distances from the audience to the work you are designing? Coupled with that, what is the conceptual framework of your audience? For example, what are the spatial limits of movements?
Do you want your audience to have a varied spatial journey themselves? Can they determine for themselves what spatial relationship they have with the work or are they guided in some way?
What is the ideal size of your audience for the work? How will you address the gap between that notional number and what you have to do work for?
In an emergency, will the audience have to evacuate around or through the work? Will safety procedures be needed to separate the work from the audience?
Do the audience themselves play a part in the work?
What are the perceptual differences occurring as a result of different distances?

Identity (Theirs)
What is the audience's history with the piece? Do they have pre-existing knowledge? Should they be confirmed in their knowledge or challenged?
What in your work depends on your audience consuming TV, cinema, the internet and other cultural references in the media? Do you think you have to share the same visual culture as your audience to convey meaning?
Where are the divisions and distinctions of your audience's visual culture in an increasingly homogenous twenty-first-century global community? Where are you in the mix?
Will your work be confusing, misrepresented (in your view) or reinterpreted in a different cultural context?
Would any of the visual jokes be lost on your audience or even cause offence?
If children are in the audience they often see things differently, in both the physical and interpretive sense – are you sure your work is appropriate for them?
What directly related media will your audience have consumed before coming? For example, will the audience have seen a video trailer of the work and what influence will that have on their subsequent experience of it, live?
Are you prepared for the 'out of body' experience of seeing your work for the first time, afresh, through the audience's eyes?

Identity (Yours)
Your audience may read a programme for the event – are you present in it? Is your biography important to include in the programme? What do you want your audience to know about yourself? Who are you writing it for? How will this 'colour' their view of your work? Would you want to show your process in the programme or would you rather focus on the resulting piece? How would an audience's knowledge of your approach affect their experience of the event?

How would you manage opening yourself up to an interview about your work?

Are you aware of your critics?

How do you handle criticism?

Who is your best critic?

Are you prepared for everyone to be a critic on social media?

Will your audience recognize your contribution within collaborative work? Do you care if they do or not?

How do you personally interact or distance yourself from your audience if you overhear comments about your work?

In a collaborative context, how would you handle your work being credited to one of your creative team and, in turn, how would you react to another's ideas in the work being credited as yours?

Diversity

Can your audience afford the cost to attend the work? How much have your audience paid and does this have an impact on what they experience? How do you address the fact that some of the audience may have paid more than others?

What is 'value for money' and what is your contribution to the audience feeling they've had it? Why would they go beyond their budget?

When you watch other works, what is your primary concern? How do you feel about other artists and designers seeing your work?

Does your audience need to have some training/education to appreciate the work?

Do you think you and your audience have different views on the past and the present?

How can wheelchair users attend the work and how might their experience differ from others because of that?

Does your work integrate practical devices for widening accessibility (e.g. surtitles, subtitles or signing)?

Is your work more attractive or interesting to one gender?

Would your family choose to see your work (if they were unrelated to you)? Would they actively choose not to go, even though they are related to you, and is that personally significant to you?

Sensitivity

Are there images that you regard as wholly inappropriate under any contextual circumstances? If so, or if not, why?

What will be the first thing your audience sees, hears, smells, touches and tastes before entering your work? Likewise, the last things when they leave?

Can everyone see/hear/smell/touch/taste the work properly?

What temperature(s) will your audience experience? How does your use of colour effect the audience's perception of that temperature?

What are your audience sitting or standing on? How does the physical sensation of what your audience are perching on, or perhaps slumped in, effect their perception and engagement, and what can you do to change that if needs be?

Are there elements in the work that require focus or concealment? If so, how do you deal with the audience's attention at any given moment?

Would you modify the work if your audience was informed that cameras, phones and other recording devices are encouraged? Can your audience suitably appreciate your work through other media?

And, finally, if you were to prioritize any of these questions, rather than categorize them, how would the tick-list change?

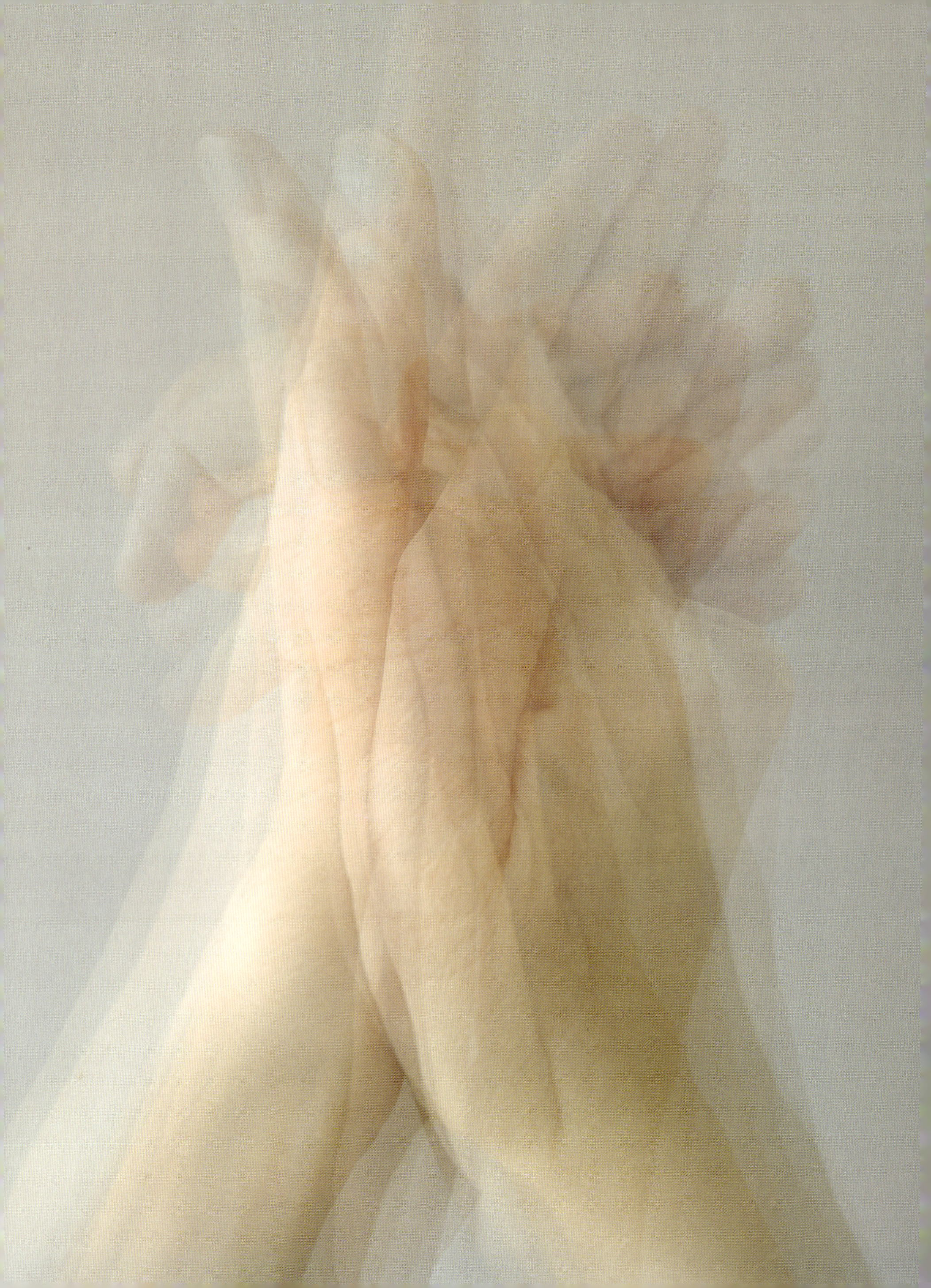

5
DOCUMENTING

Documentation is paramount to any artist whose practice is scenographic. This is because the creative work we make is collaborative and ephemeral. Collaboration requires extensive communication that is both textual and visual. To communicate design ideas during the creative process we often have to rely on documentation of research, speculations, experiments and decisions. Similarly, after the work has been created, experienced and terminated, any communication about that work requires documentation. A sketchbook should accompany you throughout the process but will any of its content make sense to you in the future? Recording the creative process and outcome with a camera ensures the survival of the captured material, but how do you then edit and organize that material for the purpose of archiving and for the possible purpose of reviving the work? Whilst it is easy to entirely immerse oneself in the present moment of every stage of the creative process, capturing every instance of it for posterity can easily lead to a confusing mass of documentation.

There is a need for us to document every step and, at the same time, organize that documentation according to its various present or future uses. To this end, it is helpful to have a pre-existing approach or framework to how one engages in research documentation differently from process documentation and from outcome documentation. Let's clarify the purposes behind each of these types of documentation, and look into different formats and structures that can be used or adapted.

OPPOSITE: *Remnants* by Leanne Vandenbussche.

RESEARCH DOCUMENTATION

Documenting research is often the only way to capture and share that research. Whilst we can describe research findings with words, this can be limiting for our interlocutors. On the other hand, a perceptual approach to capturing and sharing that research can improve our collaborators' understanding. In addition, it can allow them to perceive something else than what we perceived within the research material. Thus, a sensorial approach to documentation is conducive to a more open and interactive level of collaboration.

In many design practices, moodboards are used to collate and communicate research findings. These tend to be made of fragments of found images loosely collaged together to produce a mood or atmosphere. However, one significant issue can emerge from these moodboards. As artists and designers, we tend to be more capable of imagining an image based on two or more separate images. As an example, we may have an image of an eighteenth-century sofa and an image of a 1970s' psychedelic wallpaper that together merge in our imagination to become one clear, singular object (eighteenth-century sofa re-upholstered with 1970s' psychedelic fabric). However, our collaborators may imagine something a little, or very, different to what we have in our mind: the wallpaper might be moulded to take on the three-dimensional shape of an eighteenth-century sofa; the sofa might be re-upholstered with the wallpaper itself (rather than with a fabric where patterns have been transferred from the wallpaper); part

Spatializing Documentation

We organize the documentation of our practice for ourselves, as well as for others. The way we organize it for ourselves in the first place tends to be a less conscious effort and thus a more chaotic approach than the way we organize it for others. Yet the former approach usually informs the latter one. To this end, in order to arrange documentation for others in a way that will make sense to them, it is worth first reflecting on, and refining, the way in which we arrange it for ourselves. Now, many artists and designers whose creative practice spans across various forms and media face even more challenges in this respect: how to combine in one form/medium materials of divergent forms and media? If we can find ways to do so within the documentation we produce for ourselves, this will ease the process of re-organizing this documentation for others.

Here is a short exercise to help you reflect on, re-think and re-organize the documentation of your practice for yourself:

1. Take a photograph of your workspace (this may be as simple as a desk or include a multiplicity of furniture and surfaces, if you have a work studio of your own). The aim here is to capture in one image the environment in which all your documentation is located. If you partly document your work on a computer, it should then be featured in that photograph, probably located on your desk.
2. On an A3 sheet of paper, print this photograph at the rough size of A4 at the centre of the A3 sheet. This will provide you with a substantial white margin, or frame, all around the photograph.
3. Now you want to populate the white margins with text describing the kind of documentation dispersed in your work space. Make sure to relate these descriptions to actual elements found in the photograph by drawing lines directly from these elements to the text in the white margins. You are effectively mapping where and how you archive your practical work. In doing so, you will be able to evaluate how to streamline your approach to documenting. Indeed, it should become apparent which approaches to documentation already in use might be suitable to collate all other documentation. Conversely, it is likely that this task will reveal to you aspects of your practice that you have not been specifically archiving.
4. Repeat step 2. However, this time you are using this sheet of paper to rethink and streamline your approach to documenting. All the detailed and dispersed documentation mapped in the previous document can now be re-mapped to a lesser number of elements found in the image. If you realize that all documentation can be helpfully collated in a digital form on a computer or external hard drive, then what physical container in your workspace might be used for the archiving of the physical and analogue stuff that has been converted to a digital format? But also, how are you backing up your digital files? Remember not to keep all your documentation in only one format and at only one location.

---

of the wallpaper's psychedelic patterns might be substituted with eighteenth-century motifs (simply resulting in a hybrid wallpaper); the sofa might become a material extension of the wallpaper (where both form a continuous surface), whereby the psychedelic patterns on the wallpaper would mutate into eighteenth-century patterns, as the wallpaper starts protruding to become a sofa; and so on. Such imaginative leaps can be prone to misunderstanding. Therefore, if we are using found images, it is preferable to collage them altogether into one more or less cohesive image, or to sketch out the new image at the centre of the moodboard (surrounded by the found images). In this way, we are better supporting our collaborators' imaginative endeavours.

The found images used within the board might have initially been cut out and inserted in a sketchbook. These then would ideally be scanned and digitally integrated within the overall moodboard,

DOCUMENTING 111

Moodboard for Georg Kaiser's *From Morning to Midnight* (1912) by Keziah Drew. Note how found images are collaged together to suggest a singular environment further synthetized by the addition of drawing and a figure that provides a scale to the environment.

alongside other found images and personally produced sketches (made within the sketchbook and then, again, scanned for the moodboard). Although the moodboard thus comprises of content duplicated from the sketchbook, the particular arrangement of all this content into a moodboard should be preserved so we can return to it, if ever needed. As such, ensuring the moodboard exists in a digital format allows us to keep a record, regardless of what will happen to the physical moodboard.

As a result, when researching, we are likely to generate three types of documentation: a sketchbook, artefacts for communication (such as moodboards) and digital records of these two types of documentation. All three types will rapidly become crucial to refer to as we move forward with modelling, composing and prototyping. And these next phases of the creative process do also need to be documented. As these are more advanced forms of research, some may be documented in a sketchbook (e.g. two-dimensional compositions) but some might require another form of documentation, e.g. where should photographs of a model be documented? Some will effectively find their way in our portfolios, but how do we first collate and organize them?

PROCESS DOCUMENTATION

A sketchbook is a repository of everything that has been considered and thought through during a project. Consequently, it can be a chaotic document. So, we often have to extract and rework elements from our sketchbooks. This generates documentation outside of our sketchbook, requiring a new kind of repository. This is what might be called a project file, which is essentially a sort of portfolio dedicated to one single project. A project file helps us to edit and compile all the materials generated during a creative process. Not only will a project file ease the editing process required later on to create portfolio pages of a project, but it can also be an effective tool for a variety of creative developments.

Making work is not solely a matter of fulfilling a contract or completing a brief. In every project, our own creative and artistic development has an opportunity to grow. Of course, this is not something that a contract will stipulate, but this is something we must ensure for ourselves. And to some extent, whether we are aware or not, this creative development does take place. However, when we are not aware of it, we may not be able to nurture it as much as we would if we were more conscious of this development. First, when we keep track of, and reflect on, our creative development, we are more likely to approach every new project with the intention of establishing some scope for artistic progress. We can even set up specific goals in this respect. These goals, alongside the project's brief/framework, form the explicit and collective, as well as the implicit and personal, needs of a given project. Making a project file for every project we undertake is a strategy for reflecting on, and developing further, our creative developments.

A project file should include everything created and discovered during a project, whether or not this content has found its way into the project's outcomes. The aim of the project file is to evidence every step of the creative process. If we edit the content of the project file as the project unfolds, we might take out things that could be of relevance to future projects. Furthermore, the project file is also a useful document from which new documents can be created. Making new portfolio pages out of a multiplicity of documents and files dispersed across a range of media and formats is a longer process that runs the risk of omitting key material. A project file can be more rapidly edited to become portfolio pages or to become a proposal for a new project.

For all these reasons, a project file does not need to be laid out like a portfolio. It is a document we make for ourselves and can, therefore, have a simple layout like an edited sketchbook. However, it is not as rough as a sketchbook since it is created for the purpose of comprehensive clarity.

DOCUMENTING 113

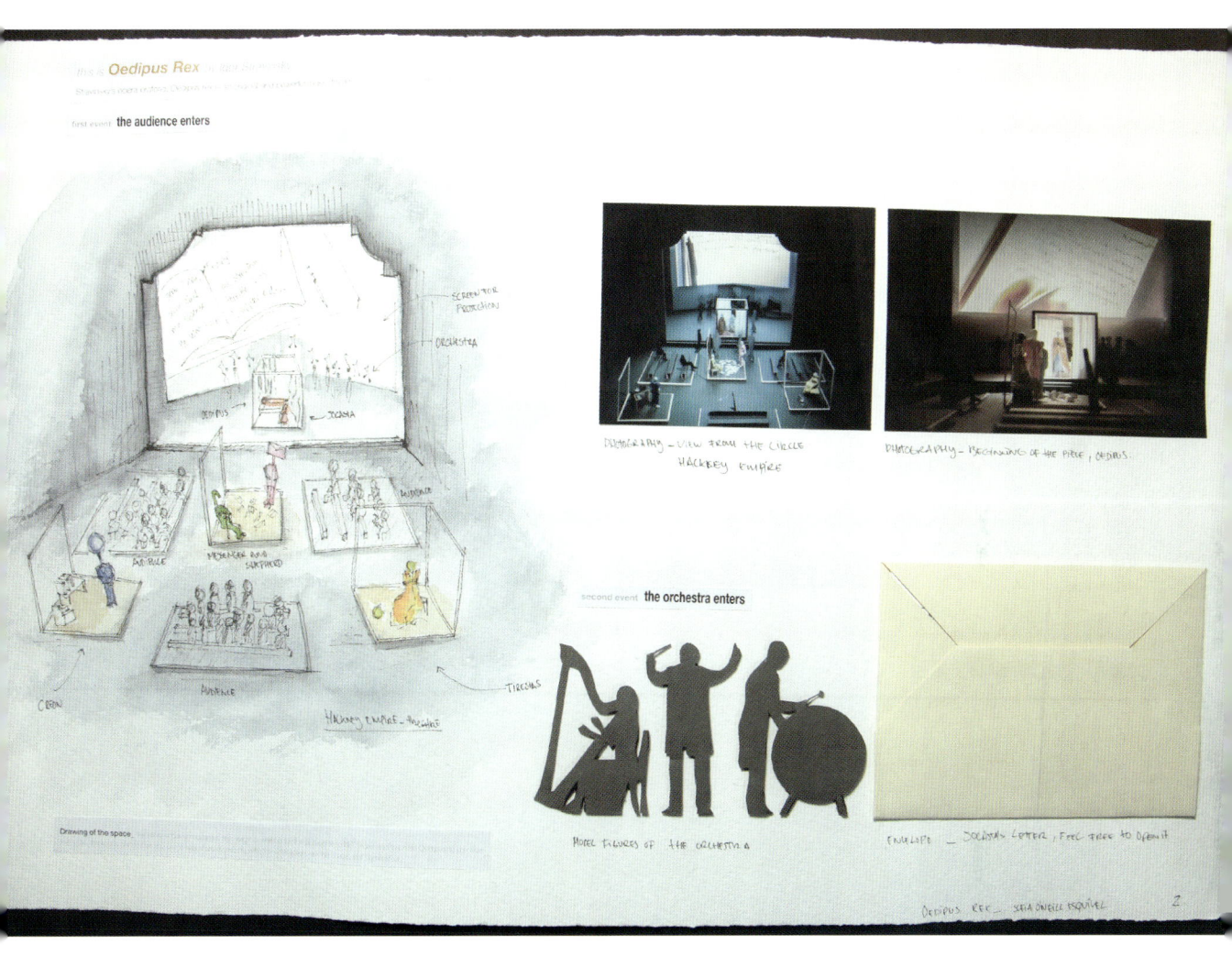

Page from project file by Sofia Esquivel. A project file compiles and organizes all the material produced during a project. It is useful for us to reflect on our creative process. It also facilitates the creation of portfolio pages effectively edited from a project file.

OUTCOME DOCUMENTATION

There are two types of outcome documentation crucial to our work, each requiring different formats and distinct processes to produce them.

We create documents for the realization of a project's outcome and for it to be repeated or recreated. These are called technical specifications. This kind of documentation is extremely precise as it is usually produced to be used by others, such as constructors, producers, curators, technical and production managers. Construction and assembly plans are some of the most common types of specifications. Such documents are not only about how the work is constructed and installed, but also how it should look. As a result, it is worth creating them in a way that both aesthetic and technical considerations run in parallel. In other words, visual documentation is placed alongside relevant technical specifications. Construction plans should be orthographic and in scale, presenting all the components and their measurements on every side of what needs to be made. Assembly plans should also show multiple views

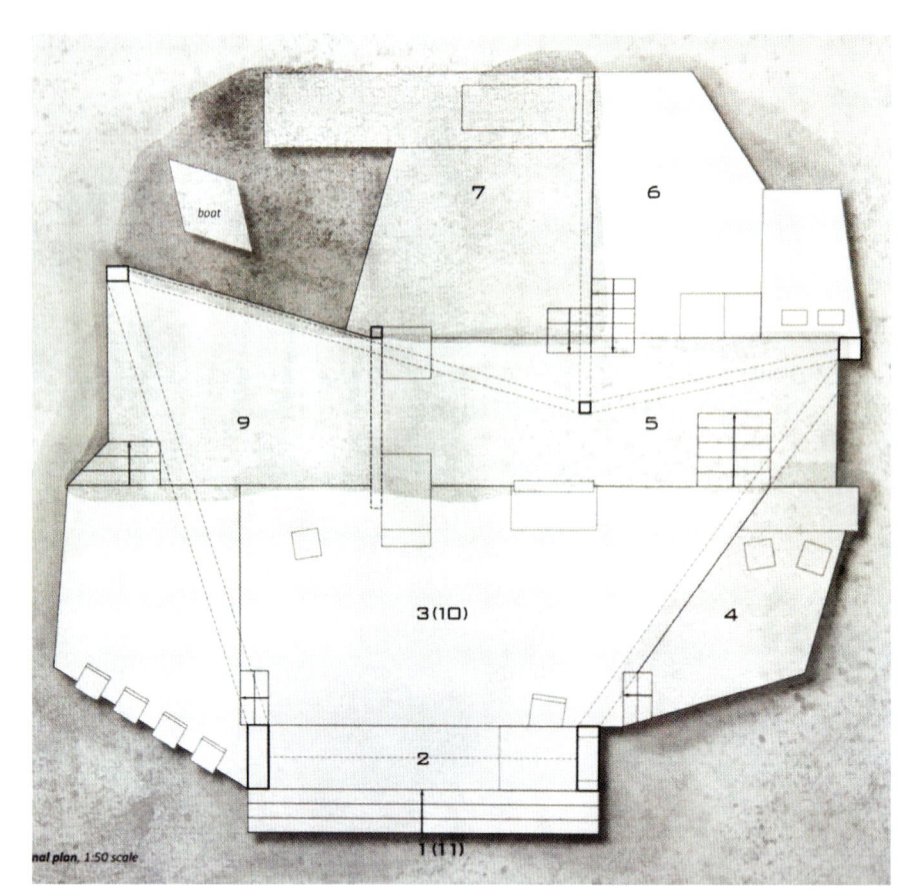

LEFT: Ground plan by Kristina Petrova. Ground plans are essential documents to finalize the positioning of material elements in space.

BELOW: Section by Sofia Esquivel. A section drawing is an elevation made by cutting through a physical structure. This section of a scenic space in a theatrical environment helps to define the exact positions of scenery with regard to the audience's sightlines (ensuring that the scenery does not block the audience's views). It is also used here to anticipate the positions of the lighting sources that will be utilized to illuminate the set.

of what needs to be assembled: ground plans, elevations and sections (which is an elevation made by cutting through an artefact), three-dimensional renderings (perspectival or axonometric) of the

RIGHT: Axonometric rendering by Sofia Esquivel. Axonometry is a type of two-dimensional representation of a three-dimensional object. An axonometric rendering provides a comprehensive view of a three-dimensional structure or object to be constructed and assembled.

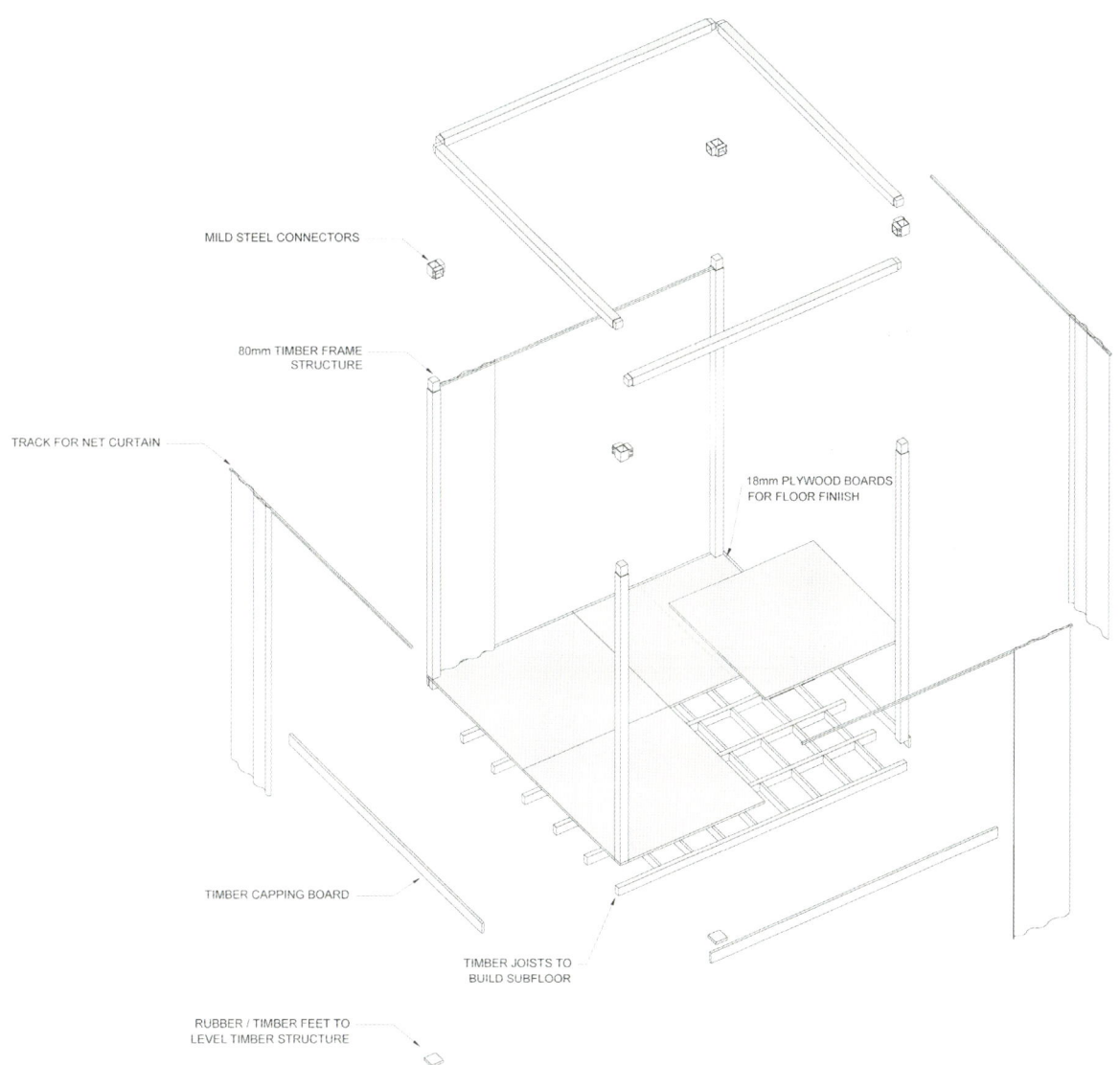

MILD STEEL CONNECTORS

80mm TIMBER FRAME STRUCTURE

TRACK FOR NET CURTAIN

18mm PLYWOOD BOARDS FOR FLOOR FINIISH

TIMBER CAPPING BOARD

TIMBER JOISTS TO BUILD SUBFLOOR

RUBBER / TIMBER FEET TO LEVEL TIMBER STRUCTURE

ABOVE: Exploded axonometric rendering by Sofia Esquivel. Exploding an axonometric rendering helps to visualize the various components of a structure or artefact before they have been connected to one another. Such rendering facilitates the processes of construction and assembly of a structure or artefact.

1:25 white card Act One

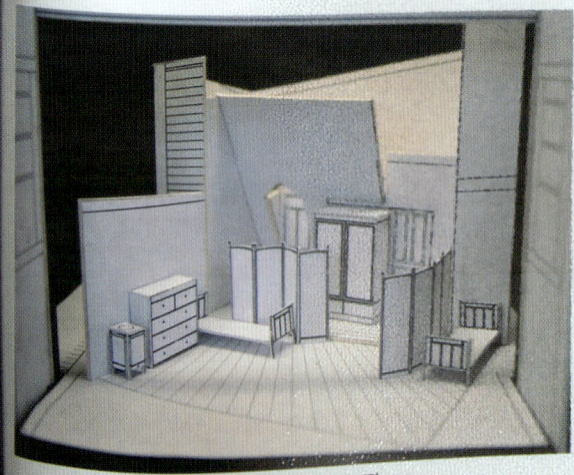

1:50 white card Act Three

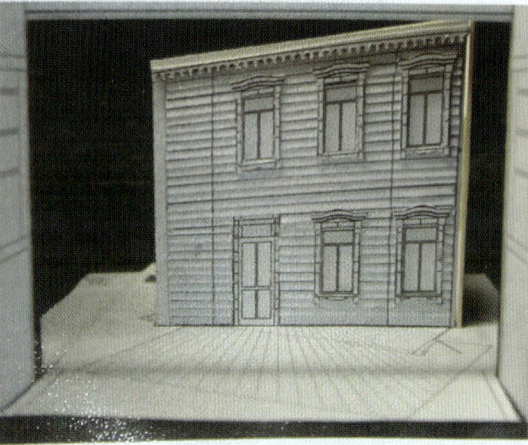

1:50 white card Act Four

assembled artefact and detailed breakdowns of the various components (particularly effective in an exploded axonometric rendering).

We document outcomes as evidences of our creative practice. This is called a portfolio. Rather than exposing the specifications of a work, portfolios re-present the work so that our creative intentions, processes and results are clarified in one document. In other words, in a portfolio we are exposing ourselves as creative individuals through the work we have made. As such, a portfolio is likely to include elements of our creative process, rather than just the results. This is because, as a form of documentation, the portfolio focuses on our personal creative outcomes, which can be found at multiple points in the process. The public outcome is certainly one of them but not the only one.

There is another reason to include elements of the process. Portfolios are used primarily to expose who we are and what we do to others who might want to work with us. While others are certainly concerned with what our completed works look like, they also tend to want to know about how we work. A portfolio, however, does not articulate a complete narrative of how the work was created nor represent the entirety of the completed work. Evidences of process in a portfolio should be edited according to the most interesting material we produced to develop the work to completion. Again, it is not about rendering the process of the work itself but highlighting our personal skills and successes within it. For instance, moment drawings can provide a helpful entry point into how the work was initiated. And white card models demonstrate an intermediate point in the process, as well as skills in three-dimensional visualization and model-making.

When bound, the way a portfolio moves from project to project, needs to follow a structure or narrative of sorts. There are many views as to how the ordering of works in a portfolio may be best achieved. Thematic ordering is useful when there is diversity in our work. For instance, thematic sections may be defined by contexts of creative practice (e.g. exhibition, events, theatre, dance, opera, TV, film, architecture or fashion) or by design areas of interest (e.g. garment, space, furniture or accessories). If your practice is equally split between independent/self-authored and collaborative projects, then your portfolio may simply be organized accordingly in two sections. Chronological and reversed chronological ordering can be considered, though reversed chronological ordering is generally preferred, as most people will want to see your most recent work first. However, such a structure will highlight the quantity and regularity (or lack of!) of your creative practice.

Portfolios do not have to be bound. Loose pages can be considered, especially if the portfolio is large (A3 and over), as this will ease the handling of the pages, which can be easily positioned on a vertical plane for a group to look at. The bigger the portfolio, the more likely it will have to be seen flat on a surface.

Here are some additional tips about portfolios:

- Landscape or portrait formats are best selected on the basis of the predominant format of the images you have. If you have a majority of landscape images, then choose a landscape portfolio.
- The larger the portfolio, the thicker the paper should be in order to avoid warping and general damages due to handling.
- Front and back cover pages should be made of a thicker and more robust paper or material, which is ideally waterproof. Laminated card is a good choice but there are a range of plastics and metals that can also be considered.

LEFT: Portfolio page with white card model by Owen Patten. Although white card models are not final models, they are worth including in a portfolio as an important phase in the creative process. On another note, portfolios increase in thickness as more and more projects are undertaken, often resulting in heavy documents, which, therefore, require strong support. Here the thickness of the cover and the plastic sleeves containing the pages will ensure longevity of the document.

- White paper gives a clean look but can be easily stained by fingerprints. When using white paper, it is advisable to use a satin-type of paper, rather than one with a matte finish, so as to make the paper less prone to fingerprints and more easily washable.
- Ring binding is most suitable for small-size portfolios (A4 and under) because, with larger portfolios, the holes on the pages will allow each page some leeway to move up or down, resulting in the pages not being perfectly aligned and, as a result of the weight and movement of the pages, the holes will be damaged over time. The paper area surrounding each hole can be strengthened but this will not fix the issue of alignment of pages.
- Prepare your digital images in view of printing: make sure they have not been compressed (you can verify this by zooming into the images: if pixilation is quickly apparent, then they were either taken in an already compressed format or they have been compressed at some point afterwards); zoom in on the edges of the image to check that the border is clean (and not concealing some distortion); crop the images according to what matters the most in the image; test print each image to check that the colour scheme is correct (there are often discrepancies between what we see on screen and what comes out in print).
- When laser printing images, consider having a slightly more satin finish to them, this will raise them slightly off the page.
- Ensure you have a convention of layout throughout the portfolio. This is particularly relevant to the first pages of each project as this convention will signal to the reader a shift to a new project. Changing conventions of layout for each project will make it confusing. Ensure there is clarity as to the end and beginning of each project.
- Try to keep all your images throughout your portfolio, at a similar kind of size. If you have a mix of small size and larger sized images, decide on just two specific sizes (small and large) and resize all the images that are slightly off these two sizes.
- Provide annotations that are as short as possible but provide additional information about an image. There is no need to annotate a drawing with the word 'drawing'. Avoid hand-writing, which can look too informal or not be legible to all. Consider font styles and font sizes that are simple and easy to read.
- Avoid including too many frames around images and texts. The paper page itself constitutes a frame within which we want to guide the reader's eyes fluidly.
- Avoid filling the page with multiple images. Allow some empty space around the images. Remember the importance of negative space in composition. But be careful not to have so much blank page that it looks like something is missing.
- An introductory page to a project should include formal information such as location, date, collaborators, name of production companies, producers and commissioning bodies.
- When an image was not taken by yourself, then make sure you credit the photographer.
- Remember that the reader is likely to look at the content of each page from left to right and from top to bottom. Order your content so that general information is read first, and the eyes of the reader are gently guided through the rest of the page.
- Include as many original drawings and sketches as possible. Portfolios are physical artefacts – their assets are found in their material and tactile dimensions. The real texture of papers and drawing materials can be advantageously provided in a portfolio. Similarly, embossing titles or including material samples help to make the portfolio more interactive.
- Consider playful and unusual formats, as this will add to the reader's experience and anchor your portfolio firmly in their memory. However, the playfulness should not distract the reader from appreciating the content, which would be rather unprofessional. Consider unusual formats that may actually solve certain problems with portfolios. For instance, portfolios can be difficult to position vertically, which can be helpful when presenting a portfolio to a group. This problem can be resolved with a playful format like concertina. In this way the portfolio is as stable vertically as it is horizontally.

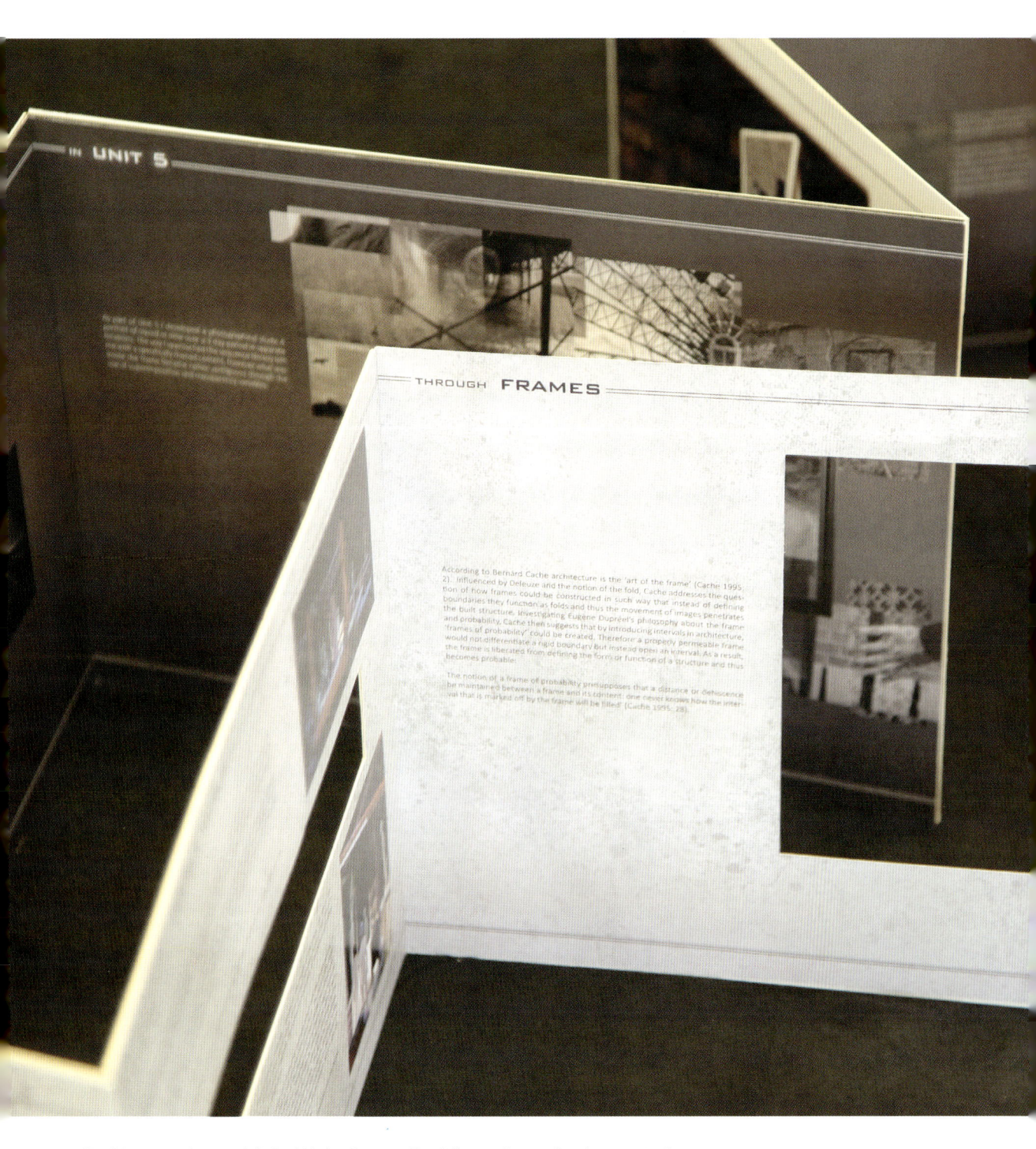

Double-concertina portfolio by Kristina Petrova. Portfolios are interactive documents: they are meant to be handled, scrutinized and questioned. As such, it is worth considering playful and unique formats (such as this concertina format) to activate dynamic interaction and make a lasting impression on the reader.

EXHIBITING SCENOGRAPHY

When re-presenting work that is scenographic in the context of an exhibition, it is almost always the case that documentation needs to used and refined to this particular end. This brings about a range of problems and challenges, as the documentation does not have the liveness, scale or three-dimensionality of the original work. However, in the context of an exhibition, the viewer is live, in real scale and situated in a three-dimensional space. Thus, in many ways, the viewer is in a similar position as the original audience was, but the work is no longer experienced under these conditions. For this reason, exhibiting scenographic work is not straightforward. How can the experiential dynamics of performance (environmental, embodied and ephemeral) be represented in the exhibition space? Although this question raises all sorts of challenges, it is simultaneously of paramount importance to the museological world at present. Indeed, as mentioned before, the museum audience is a live, dynamic and physically present entity. Museological environments have realized the importance of engaging their audience in these exact terms, as this provides a more dynamic and enriching experience. Regardless of the kind of content they are presenting, museums are seeking to make it more accessible and impactful by engaging their viewers in immersion, participation and interaction. This provides a more flexible and appropriate framework for exhibiting documentation of scenographic work. How then can drawings, scale models and prototypes be exhibited so as to have a spatial and timely impact on the viewer? The answers to this question revolve around how these documents can physically and perceptually relate to the viewer. Drawings can be presented in such a way that the viewer's body has to actively engage with a spatial structure that contains or conceals the drawings. Their size may also be enlarged so as to become a spatial feature. Scale models can be animated for a camera to be presented as films. They can also be modified and extended to become part of the viewer's space.

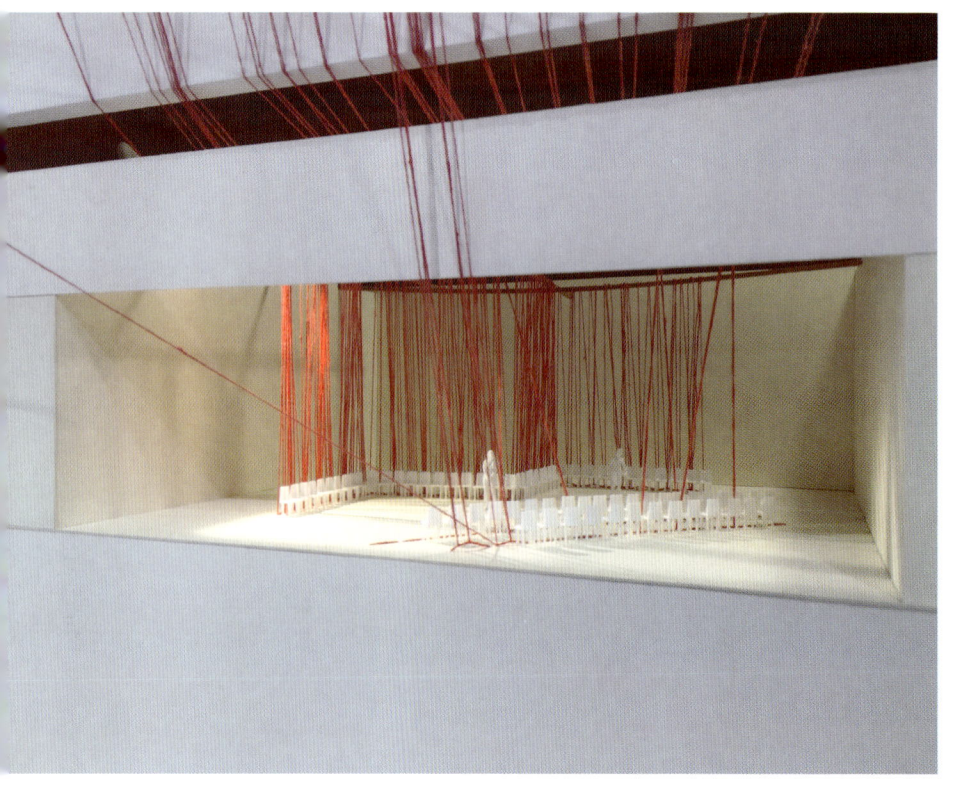

Scale model installation by Wenjiao Wang. In the context of an exhibition, how can scenographic documentation be presented so as to continue engaging the viewer with the potential of a live event? For instance, a scale model is performative not merely because it represents a performance environment of sorts, but because it is physically manipulated during a creative process. Thus, in the context of an exhibition we might consider presenting models as interactive artefacts (rather than static objects). This is likely to require transforming some aspects of the model. But other tactics can be considered too. Here, key aspects of the spatial design found in the model (audience immersed in a stage space defined by chairs and red strings) have been extended beyond the model and into the viewer's space.

Scale model installation by Wenjiao Wang. An important part of the design presented in this model is extended into the space of the visitor to create a more immersive experience and a tactile desire to interact (here to pull the strings).

PROFESSIONAL INSIGHT

Photographing
Jemima Yong

Jemima Yong is a performance maker, photographer and puppeteer. Collaboration, experimentation and interdisciplinarity are central to her practice. She is part of the performance collective JAMS, recipient of The Oxford Samuel Beckett Theatre Trust Award 2018. Previously, she has co-run National Art Service with Alan Fielden and has toured work to France, Russia and Singapore.

Camera Settings
Set your digital camera to manual mode – this will allow you to adjust settings that affect the brightness, contrast, depth of field, texture and colour of your photograph. Changing one variable at a time, familiarize yourself with the effects of each setting.

- Shutter speed: this is measured in seconds. Keep this fast, if you want your subject to be captured sharply. Slow it down, if you want your photograph to trace the subject's or your camera's movement. The faster the shutter speed, the darker the image. This can be compensated by increasing the ISO or widening the aperture.
- ISO: the higher the number, the more sensitive the camera is to light. The more sensitive it is to light, the brighter and 'noisier' the image.
- Aperture: this is the circular opening through which light enters the camera. The number correlates to the thickness of the aperture's circumference. The smaller the number, the thinner the circumference, the wider the circle; more light is able to enter, and the resulting image is brighter.
- Aperture also affects the image's depth of field, which manifests as the variance of sharpness between the sharpest plane in your image and its surroundings. A large number is appropriate if you want your entire image sharp. The

RIGHT: An image from SUN, a site-specific performance produced and photographed as part of National Art Service. SUN was written and directed by Alan Fielden and staged at St Leonard's Church in 2014.

(continued overleaf)

(continued from previous page)

smaller the number, the more contrast there is between the sharpness of the sharpest plane of your image and its surroundings.

Picture style and white balance settings alter the colours in your image:

- Picture style: Custom make your own picture style – what are you drawn to in relation to sharpness, contrast, saturation and colour tone? How do different picture styles bring out different qualities in the photograph and how does this relate to the live performance?
- White balance setting: altering your white balance helps your image counteract the colour temperature of your light source, so that what you perceive as white with your eyes is also rendered white on the photograph. If you customize your white balance, you are telling the camera what is white in the image; every other colour is then rendered in relation to that. White balance is measured in Kelvin (K). The larger the number, the 'warmer' the image; the smaller the number, the 'colder' the image.

When photographing performance, I like keeping my camera on continuous shooting mode, so I can photograph in phrases.

Things to Consider Before and While You Shoot

Function

- What is the purpose of the photograph?
- Who are the intended viewers of the image?
- What is the difference between a photograph for the company's archive, a photograph to publicize the performance and a photograph for your portfolio?

Perspective

- How you move with the camera affects the outcome of the image. I tend to keep my eye to the viewfinder. The smaller the gap between my body and the camera, the more control I feel over the image outcome. What happens to your experience of taking the photograph when

LEFT: Another image from SUN.

(continued overleaf)

(continued from previous page)

you compose the image by looking at the display screen? Perhaps this is preferable?
- Sometimes the camera can immobilize the body. Bear in mind, the zoom is not your only available movement.
- What does the performance look like from above you? How does it look from below you?
- What would a fly on the wall see? What would the ceiling see?
- Find fresh eyes – assume a vantage point from which the performance is not designed to be experienced. Observe it from this different angle. Making the subject unfamiliar, what new things are discovered?

Performance

- Typically, live performance encompasses movement and low light – anticipate this. Lenses that have large apertures and fast shutter speeds are suitable here. Depending on your contribution to the work and when you are photographing, you may or may not be able to request more light.
- How steady are your hands?
- How can alternating your breath help you achieve the photograph you want? What happens when you mimic the breath of your subject?
- Catching 'the climax' – the sound playing can tell you a lot about the scene. What else can give you a sense of what is happening or what is about to happen?
- What are the themes of the performance? What is its essence? How can these translate into your photographs?
- Do you want to plan what images you want to take? Is there a checklist of scenes you are anticipating? It can be useful to write down what you definitely want to photograph. It can also be useful to respond in the moment and discover as you shoot.
- How does photographing in colour and photographing in monochrome alter the way the image is viewed and the way you interact with the live performance?

Focus

- What is the focus of the performance? What is the focus of the photograph? Do they have to be the same thing?
- Can there be more than one point of focus?
- Explore multiple ways of establishing focus beyond the sharpness of the subject in relation to its surroundings.
- What is the relationship between the subject and the space around him or her?

Liveness

- When is the best time to shoot? Are you in a dress rehearsal, a technical rehearsal or a photocall?
- Familiarize yourself with the space in which you are photographing. What kind of floor does it have? Do your shoes make a lot of noise on it? Would you prefer to be in bare feet?
- What is your relationship to the subject? Do you want them to know you are there? Do you want them to forget you are there? What is your relationship to other people in the space? Adjust your presence accordingly.
- Be sure you know what the limits of your mobility are – how close/how far can you be from the performers?
- What part of the performance is being performed for you to photograph? Where does this take place in the arc of the full performance?
- I try not to photograph performances on show nights. Cameras are noisy and distracting to audiences and performers. It can also limit the number of vantage points I am able to shoot from. Sometimes it is not possible to shoot before a show. Adjust your presence in the space accordingly.
- Is the image you're looking for going to be created in post-production through, say, a crop? If this is the case, consider taking a wider shot than you need.

Lighting

- Where is the light coming from?
- Where do you want it to come from?
- Can you move to a point in the space where the light is coming from the direction you want it to come from?
- Theatre works on contrast – light balance is not always what you want.
- Where are the shadows?
- Where are the reflections?
- What might a live audience miss? What might a live audience see?

An image taken by a participant of Here's the Thing, a commissioned audio-visual installation created in collaboration with composer-educator Timothy Cape and twenty-six 9-year-olds for the International Youth Arts Festival in Kingston, 2016.

- When will you need a tripod? Is it important for you to be able to move around? How can you use what's available to substitute for a tripod?

Composition exercise
The rule of thirds is a visual composition guideline. It proposes that an image should be composed to a grid that splits the frame up into nine equal parts and that placing important elements of the image within the lines or on the intersections makes for a more pleasing image.
What you need:

- An A4 frame (without the hard back or the glass).
- Four rubber bands.

Tie two rubber bands across the horizontal plane of the frame and two rubber bands round the vertical plane of the frame. Space them out evenly so you end up with a rectangle split into nine equal portions.

- Explore your environment through the frame. Take time to be precise about what you want to include and what you want to exclude. Consider how the important elements of your image sit within, or on, the intersections of the lines. What feels satisfying to you?
- Switch the frame for your camera.
- Capture what you can see.
- Then capture what you can't see.

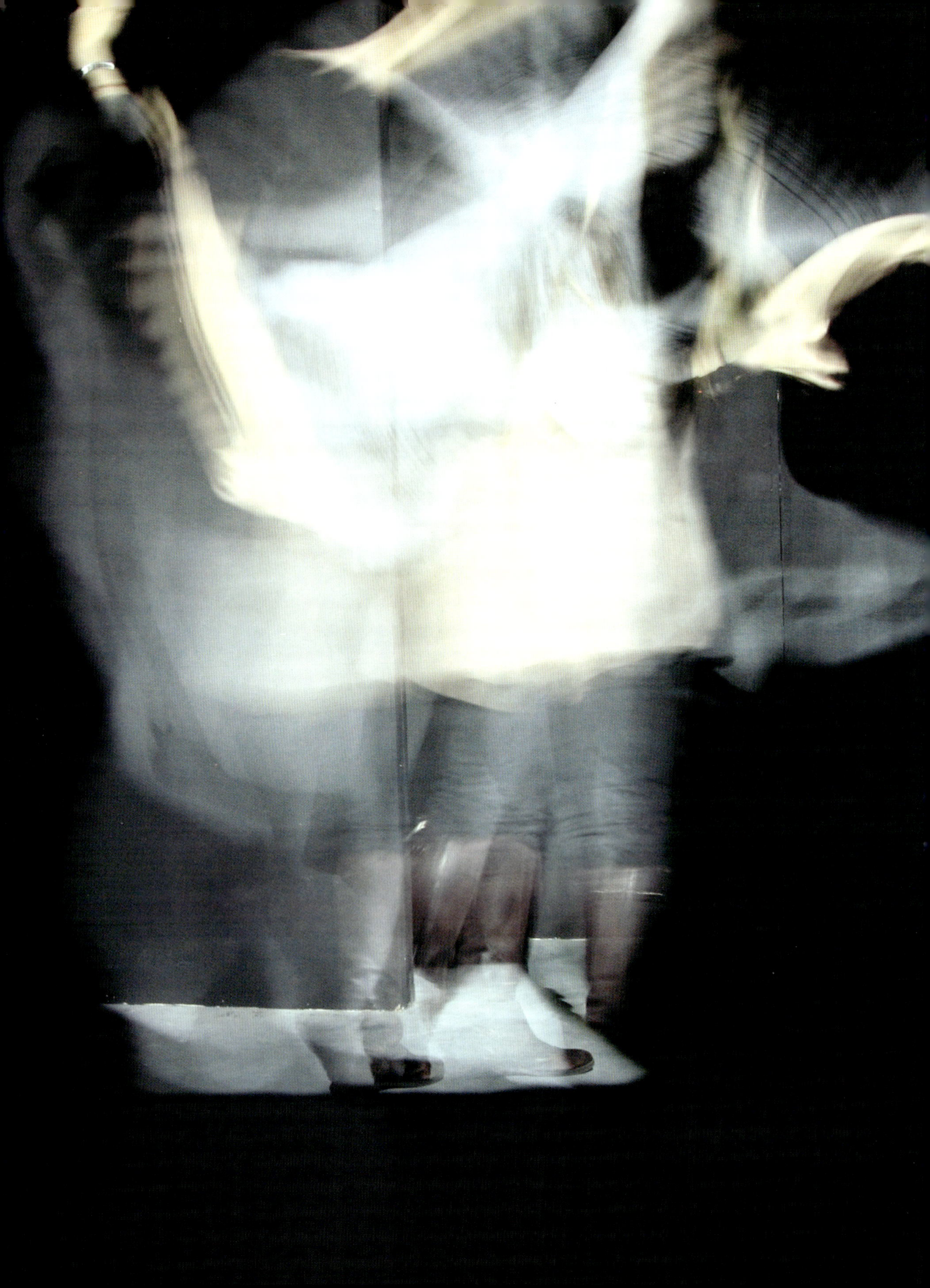

6
RESEARCHING

What is research in a practical context such as scenography? Commonly understood as the initial phase of a creative process, research is an active engagement with questioning and discovering new things, such as information, ideas, visual forms and practical processes. Through research we pose new questions to learn something new, which we can then translate and develop in practice: hence the expression research and development (R&D). Typically, research and development occurs at the start of a project. This implies that at some point in the project, research will cease. However, the entire creative process from beginning to end can be a form of research if we allow ourselves to keep discovering and developing from these discoveries until the work is completed. In this case, our approach to research is likely to be less directed at first and more focused later on.

In this chapter, I present a case study of personal research that precisely moves from initially loose directions undertaken in a laboratory context of practical experimentation, to highly focused intentions in public contexts of professional practice. Just as importantly, the case study will provide an instance of how analysis and reflection can support the transition from historical and conceptual findings to practical discoveries.

INITIAL QUESTIONS

The research started from a personal interest in negative spaces, resulting from the fact that my eyes are particularly attracted to darkness due to being rather sensitive to bright light. Traditionally, scenography revealed visual content by concealing its mechanisms in line with how the stage is a platform of exposure that required hidden areas. Historically, multiple devices have been created to conceal: trap doors to hide things under the stage, curtains and borders to hide things around and above the stage. These can be seen as negative spaces because, although they are peripheral and not integrated in the composition on stage, they frame it in a way that audiences are aware of it. In light of this dependency of the stage image on its concealed framework, I perceived the all-encompassing darkness of the black box theatre as a radical exposure of the presence of the negative space. I wondered what might have enabled the negative space's historical transition from the hidden to the visible.

This initial question led to the work of performance artist Loie Fuller, who used her own performing body as a negative space. Fuller used slide projections on a most unusual costume, which she patented in 1894. Sometimes white (*Fire Dance* 1895, *Ballet of Light* 1908), sometimes black (*Firmament and Night* 1896), Fuller's gigantic draped outfit simultaneously functioned as both a screen and a set that she would animate by way of spinning her body around. In addition, Fuller designed discrete scenic panels made of reflective

OPPOSITE: Wearable Shadows

materials, located on horizontal and vertical planes of the stage, to reflect and multiply the unfathomable presence of the moving drapery. As a result, Fuller's own body was barely perceivable within, and due to, the mass of fabric (and its reflections) moving from, and around, her body. The movement of her body modulated the visual perception of both its costume and its surrounding volume of space. At the same time, the material nature of the costume affected how her body moved as it challenged her body's proprioceptive skills (balance).

There are two aspects of Fuller's scenography that were interesting to interrogate because of their relevance to, and divergence from, contemporary practices:

- The body's immersive engagement with technology: Fuller's fusion of body and technology relates to, and differs from, our contemporary engagement with digital culture. Whereas digital technologies tend to immerse the body in two-dimensional imagery, Fuller used her body as a screen to force the two-dimensionality of the projected image into a three-dimensional and physical phenomenon. In contemporary performance design, the inclusion of projection on stage can flatten and disrupt the visual perception of the live performing body. Thus, it is often the case that projection is used to create a background so that it has a distinct position separate from performers. Developing Fuller's innovation in light of contemporary practice could enable further understanding of how projection can be dynamically integrated on the live and three-dimensional body. Since Fuller experimented with, and modified, the projection technologies of her time in order to create her work, research would probably need to engage in an innovative use of contemporary technologies of projection. And as with Fuller's work, the challenge then would also be related to adapting the body's movement to explore that integrated relationship without losing complete sight of the body's live presence.
- The visual phenomenon of the environment dominates over the visual perception of the performer: much unlike any performance traditions, Fuller's work augments the presence of the scenography and reduces the visibility of the performer to near disappearance. The body is core to the action on stage, but its presence is dissolved by this very staged action. Therefore, there is an affirmation of the traditional function of scenography and, at the same time, a subversion of it since scenography was used to frame and highlight the body. Furthermore, Fuller would require the lighting that illuminated her audience to be turned off so as to further dissolve the border between auditorium and stage. The visual uncertainty layered over what is otherwise a highly structured environment, then seems to anticipate the black box theatre that emerged a few decades later. Indeed, the black box space is inherently lacking a visual order of distinction between stage, off-stage and auditorium. As such, developing Fuller's unique approach to intersecting the body and technology further should be facilitated by locating these developments within a black box environment.

Dramaturgically, Fuller's performances' titles referred to natural phenomena, clearly affirming a desire to translate exterior and non-human events into interior and man-made situations. This explains in part why her work attempts at disturbing the perception of the architectural structure in which it takes place. More importantly, this further reflects her desire to erase divisions between stage and its surrounding, between an inside and an outside, a focal point and its periphery. Now, the black box environment is already one that has no specific order of stage and auditorium. Therefore, to explore the scenographic tension between interior and exterior environments, I chose dramaturgical stimuli related to man-made and ordered domestic spaces. These spaces are elaborated on the premise of particular positions and locations of the body. How could these be visually dissolved by way of translating them in the black box space through the use of technologies?

INITIAL PRACTICE

I started with a series of drawings speculating about interactions between bodies and projection, in the black box, using everyday spatial elements as stimuli to be perceptually dissolved by the aforementioned interactions. I undertook to draw situations in which the bodies are distinctively positioned yet digital projection phenomena confound and disperse their positions. In doing so, as I am about to analyse, the speculative drawings led me to envision a paradoxical type of lighting phenomenon, which would drive the next phase of practice. Here I will present and discuss the drawings that most significantly bear on the process of advance towards that next phase.

Speculative drawing #2 The Dressing Room. At the beginning of these series of drawings, I speculated about situations where the black box environment is utilized to disperse bodies' location in space: here light and projection are used to cast doubles of the bodies on walls.

Speculative drawing #6 *The Glass Door*. In this drawing, I speculate about a situation in the black box where a hanging screen would separate two bodies in space yet still allow for each body to perceive the other by way of capturing and projecting a live image of each body on either side of the screen. How would they interact with one another?

Speculative drawings #2 *The Dressing Room* and #6 *The Glass Door* demarcate clear positions for the physical presence of one performer and one audience member. Respectively, using the black box's own walls and a gauze as projection screens, these situations use video projection to mirror and superimpose the performer's and audience's bodies live in order to enable their movements to unfold dialogically – as in a duet – though making it impossible for either one to clearly perceive the other. Importantly here, the projection surface is not the focal point for the audience's perception, as they can also perceive or sense some aspect of the performer's actual presence in space (behind the audience member in *The Dressing Room* and behind the gauze in *The Glass Door*). In this way, both sketches speculate on the kinetic relation and interaction of two bodies (performer and audience) by way of positioning the performer as a double of the audience: the

Speculative drawing #11 *The Bedroom*. Here a projection screen is hanged horizontally, parallel to the floor, where one body would be lying down yet perceiving itself suspended in the air above itself. The live projection double of this body would be visually manipulated and distorted to test out the impact on the movement of the actual body.

performer's location in space functions as a kind of shadow of the audience. How then would these two bodies move in this remote duet?

Speculative drawings #11 *The Bedroom* and #12 *The Wall* only include one body because the body's double is now a live-fed projection of itself, animated within the projection. Further, the spatial positions and material conditions given to the body induce movement and are visually responsive in different ways. In *The Bedroom*, the body is required to lie down in order to face a suspended image of themselves on a hanging screen. This dual positionality is further disrupted by another perception of its distorted double found within the reflective and circular edges of the bed. In *The Wall*, the body is required to engage with an unevenly curved climbing wall-screen within which its distorted double is projected. Here, no particular focal point is implemented, since the proximity between the body and its projected double, as well

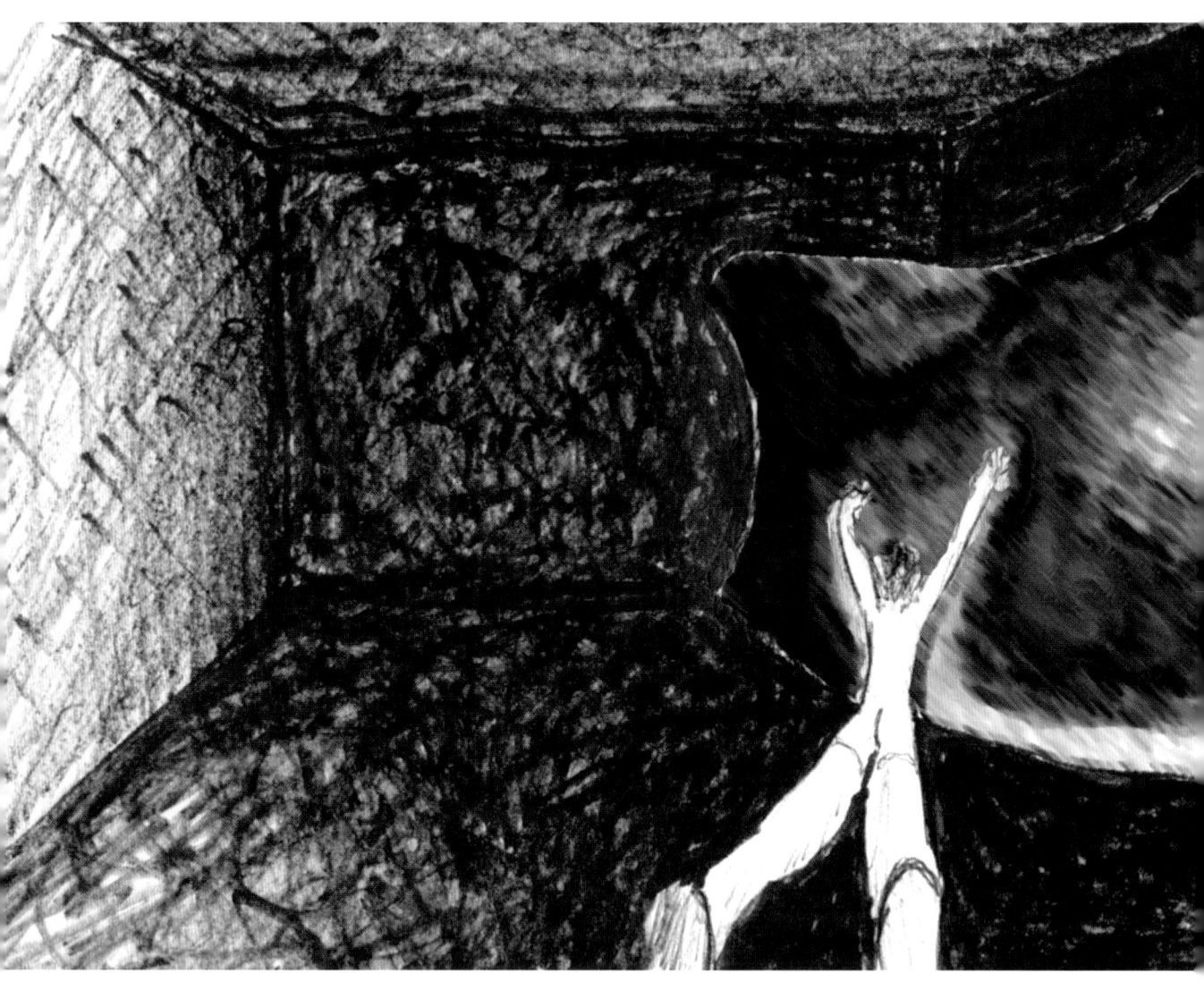

Speculative drawing #12 *The Wall*. Here a large black reflective surface forms a climbing wall: how would a body climb distorted reflections of itself?

as the distorting curves of the wall, force the body to shift its visual attention constantly across the surface of the wall. Thus, in both cases, the body's position in space is disturbed by both projection and spatial structures. How then would the body behave and move in relation to its disorienting projected double?

Subsequently, I endeavoured to speculate on ways to further explode the body's position in space by reflecting fragments of itself throughout its surroundings. To do so, I chose to transpose everyday spaces that are perceptually disorienting. Speculative scenario #15 *The Shower Room* is the best example of this last phase of the series in that it sparked the next phase. Importantly, this sketch does not include a body, for the positioning and movement of the body had become highly uncertain.

In shower rooms, water droplets and steam occupy all surfaces, as well as the spatial volume. The attenuation of visual clarity in these environments provokes unstable perceptual and physical experiences to occur. I thus conceived of a

Speculative drawing #15 *The Shower Room*. No body is present here because there is no expected position or location for the body in this speculative situation. Small fragments of screens are hanging throughout the volume of the space. Each shows a small part of an overall projection that covers the entire space. The content of the projection is live: the projector is connected to a camera that captures any body present in the space. A body could exist and travel anywhere in the space, but at every movement all the hanging bits of screens would display shifting portions of that body. So how would a body move in a space which is like a cloud of moving fragments of itself? This speculative situation led me to consider whether projection alone (without any screens) could interact with the body and, as such, orient it in space.

constellation of suspended fragments of screens dispersed throughout the volume of a black box. Again live-stream digital media would capture, project and explode the presence of the body on to the micro-screens, parts of the walls and floor and on the body itself. The emphasis on an exploded volumetric space and the inspiration coming from steam and water falling down make this sketch most relatable to a Fuller-like scenario. However, here there is no requirement of a particular position in space for the work to unfold. Thus, the body can travel anywhere across the space. But how would the body move within this cloud of fragments of reflections of itself?

Importantly, in *The Shower Room* the floor is free from spatial structures, thus reducing material additions in space to allow more freedom for the body to move. The reduction of tangible materials in space led to considering the removal of the suspended fragments of screens and incorporating this fragmentation within projection itself. Evidently this would provoke a complication to the media content required to realize such a situation experimentally, as it meant that the content would not be distorted by physical pieces of screen but would have a pre-existing structure of fragmentation. Conceptually, the progressive move from projecting digital media on to flat surfaces to dispersing it more and more into the volume of space can be formulated as a way of returning projection to what it really is: light, as a phenomenon that permeates volumetric space before ending at a surface.

Thus, I concluded the first phase of practice with questions of light pertaining to my sketch *The Shower Room*. This drawing speculated on the possibility of projected phenomena behaving as a fragmented light beam, which every piece reflects and reacts to the body. This speculative scenario sought to expand light's behaviour within a disorienting form. This is a kind of inversion of light's function, since its usual purpose is to clarify visual content and support orientation. I was starting to conceive of a lighting phenomenon that would alone create the visual fragmentation that Fuller explored by the intersection of moving costume and projected content.

INTERMEDIATE DEVELOPMENTS

Through further historical research, I discovered that the questions I was asking could be found, after Fuller, in the works of some Bauhaus artists. On the Bauhaus stage, the movement of performing bodies was challenged and fragmented by scenographic devices, such as costumes, props and scenery. László Moholy-Nagy's *Light Prop* (1930) constitutes such a device in the realm of lighting and projection. *Light Prop* was conceived as a lighting source whose moving parts and grids would disperse and animate fragments of light and shadows (including the body's) on stage. Although *Light Prop* was a lighting source, the fact that it also casted moving shadows of various forms, thereby creating visual content such as grids and fragments of bodies' shadows, makes it a projection tool of sort. This object blurs the technical boundaries between light and projection. Let's be clear, strictly speaking projection is light. The differentiation between light and projection is made on the basis of the purpose of the visual phenomenon and its related structure: projection offers intangible content that is more clearly perceived when established on a flat surface; therefore, a projector is structured so as to control the direction of the light beam to contain it on a screen; lighting illuminates tangible content that is often achieved by the structure of the light source, which diffuses the light beam in space. Yet, as a lighting source, *Light Prop* does not illuminate tangible content in a stable way; and, as a projector, the object did not offer clear intangible content, since it is moving and distorted by the environment. In this respect, Moholy-Nagy's device produced the kind of visual phenomena Fuller had created, whilst only using a light source as I had come to consider through my drawings. As a result, I was keen to further develop *Light Prop* with respect to contemporary technologies of projection used as a light source, though neither illuminating the tangible space nor exposing intangible content.

Operative drawing #7. Hand-drawing made with a view to being projected in a black box space. Once projected, the space was just very bright: I could not see, or interact with, the details of the drawing.

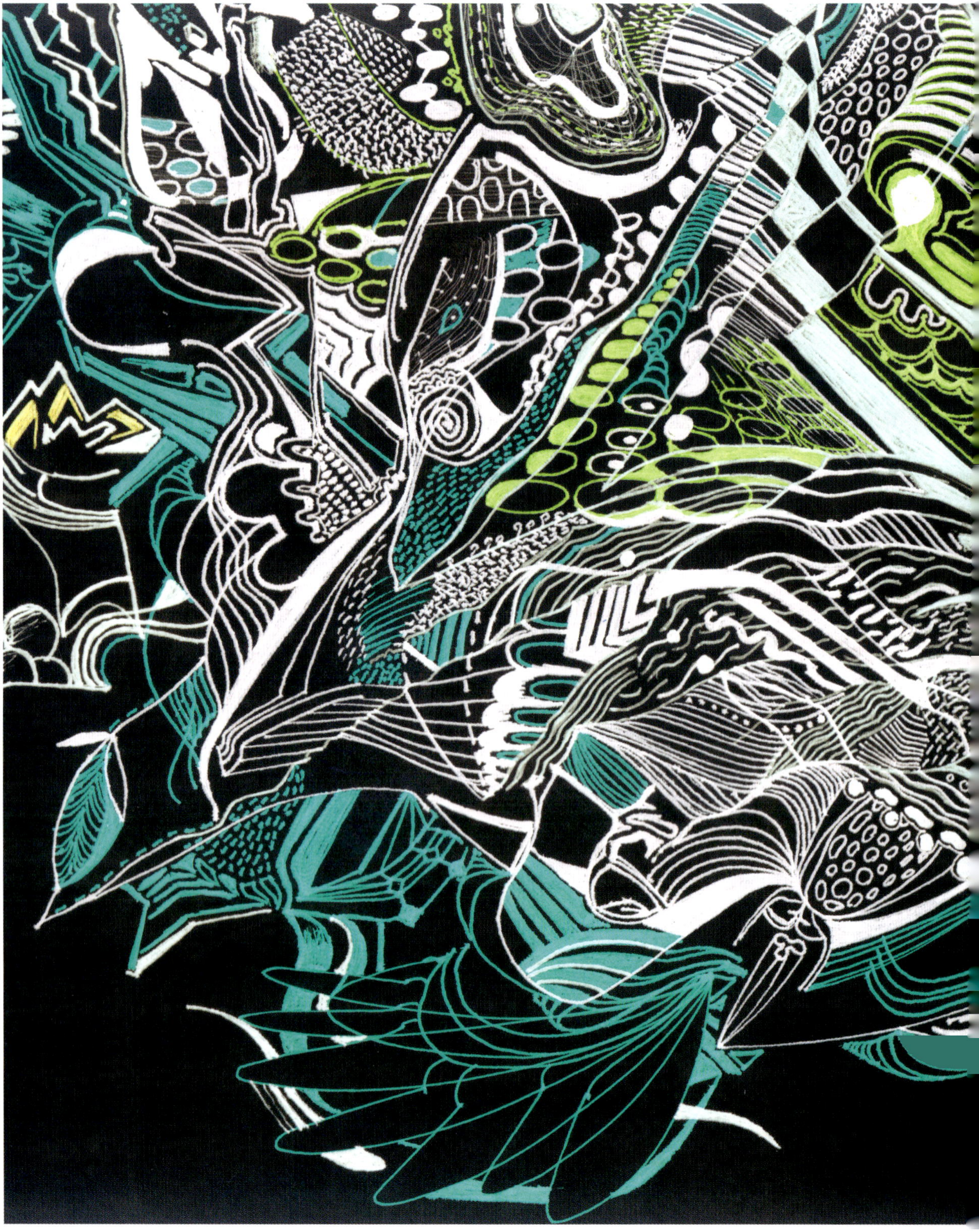

For this reason, I first considered using a digital projector to project a fragmented image over the entire space of a black box in such way that neither the image nor the black box would be visually revealed. To this end, I produced a series of handmade operative drawings that I aimed to process digitally in order to project them in a space that I could then try to inhabit. Each drawing was thus conceived as a projected field of light with greater or lesser fragmentation. This time, my drawing approach had more precise rules. Since these drawings would become a field of light in space for my body to tentatively move into, I needed their fragmentation to be as unpredictable as possible. In this way, I hoped that I would somehow rediscover these images once projected in space (rather than already know and move according to their overall structure). Thus, I opted for a scaffolded operative strategy of drawing: a 'directional lability [, a] lacework [,] branchwork stimulating' (Robertson 2003: 165). I drew one motif at a time, each motif growing out of the previous one, or any other form near or in contact with it. I would repeat the motif in a loose chain-like structure until it would become almost automatic for my hands to draw it, at which point I would morph the motif (e.g. change colour, size, texture or form) and change the direction of the branch or create a new branch. In this way, I could prevent the emergence of a central area, a dominating core or a pre-eminent singular direction, as well as randomly balance the distribution of filled and empty areas.

The first drawings of the series present complex arrays of textures and colours because I was translating in drawing all the possible qualities of the radiant energy that is light and that are replicated by theatrical lighting equipment: direction, angle, intensity, focus, form, colour and texture. In addition, I first made use of the whiteness of the paper page to create gaping fragments that were conceived as negative spaces. However, as I implemented the drawings' projection in a black box,

LEFT: Operative drawing #14. Digitally inverted version of operative drawing #7, once projected in space, I could perceive far too many details to be able to interact with them.

my body's immersion into them found it impossible to interact with the complexity of motifs, as I could not discriminate them from the white gaps: both were bright and thus the space was entirely flooded with light. As a result, I inverted the drawings' background and gaps to black (even though the projector still emits light in these black gaps, the intensity of their brightness is much lower than white and much less sensed by the immersed body, which could, as a result, more easily pinpoint and engage with the brighter motifs).

Projected in a black box space, these more contrasted drawings facilitated a stronger engagement on my body's part. I explored how I could move within, and according to, their specificities by following a strict routine: using a laptop, I would operate a slideshow of the drawings, activate the link between computer and digital projector, switch on the record button of the video camera and walk into the portion of black box space flooded by the projection. After moving through the projection, I would return to the camera to pause the recording, rewind it, play and watch it, until reaching where I had paused and stop it (ready for the next recording). I would then walk to the computer's desk to move to the next slide, the next drawing, then walk back to the camera to push 'record' again, and walk back into the new projection, back and forth. First-hand experiences from within offered two separate, yet correlated, findings:

- Facing the projector, I observed the drawings imprinted upon my body, an inward gazing that slowed my body down to quasi-stillness. Although the drawings were static, when observing them on my body, they started moving to my movements: every tiny movement on my part shifted and seemingly animated the drawing on the three-dimensional surface of my body. As I accelerated my movements, the drawings were further distorted, flickering up to become fuzzy and unspecified, which made paying attention to them quite a dizzying experience. Similarly, when gazing directly at the projector's shining lens, I was slightly blinded but I could sense, rather than see, the drawing: my eyes felt degrees of heat relevant to the intensity of the part of the drawing I was passing through. That is to say, I only felt whether I was passing through dark areas of the drawing (low heat over my eyes) or bright areas (high heat, almost painful, over my eyes): an oscillation between two differing degrees of blindness.
- Turning my back to the projector I could no longer see the drawings imprinted upon my body but, lightly or strongly, cast around my own shadow against the black wall of the space. This position suddenly shifted the perception of space towards an elusive sense of depth, as the projections made the wall appear semi-transparent, as if I could go through it, which would often fool my body into creating large movements that were cut painfully short by the wall.

Through these experiments, I was increasingly able to identify visual qualities in the projection content with which I could physically interact: small, simple and bright motifs were most effective, as I could perceive them and their apparent movements. Thus, I went back to drawing, producing new and simpler compositions that I further simplified through digital means: increasingly cancelling the variety of forms, colours and textures to retain, in the end, only a few white pixels, organized through a multiplicity of directions and intensities (brightness). I would also ensure that these pixels would still form corridors and pathways, so as to be able to test out whether my body would be able to perceive and follow these implicit trajectories.

Once projected, these drawn fields of white pixels could be easily perceived on all the surfaces of the space in such a way that I could intentionally bring my body into them, seemingly to capture them and make them move. Perceptually, then, my gaze would always return to my own body. Furthermore, once a motif was overlapping an area of my body, I would instinctively start moving that area to distort the motif and make it slide on to another body part that would then become the new focus of movement. My body was thus

Operative drawing #18. I continued simplifying the drawings by eliminating colours and forms, reducing them to just white and grey lines. When projected, I could easily perceive and follow them as navigational routes.

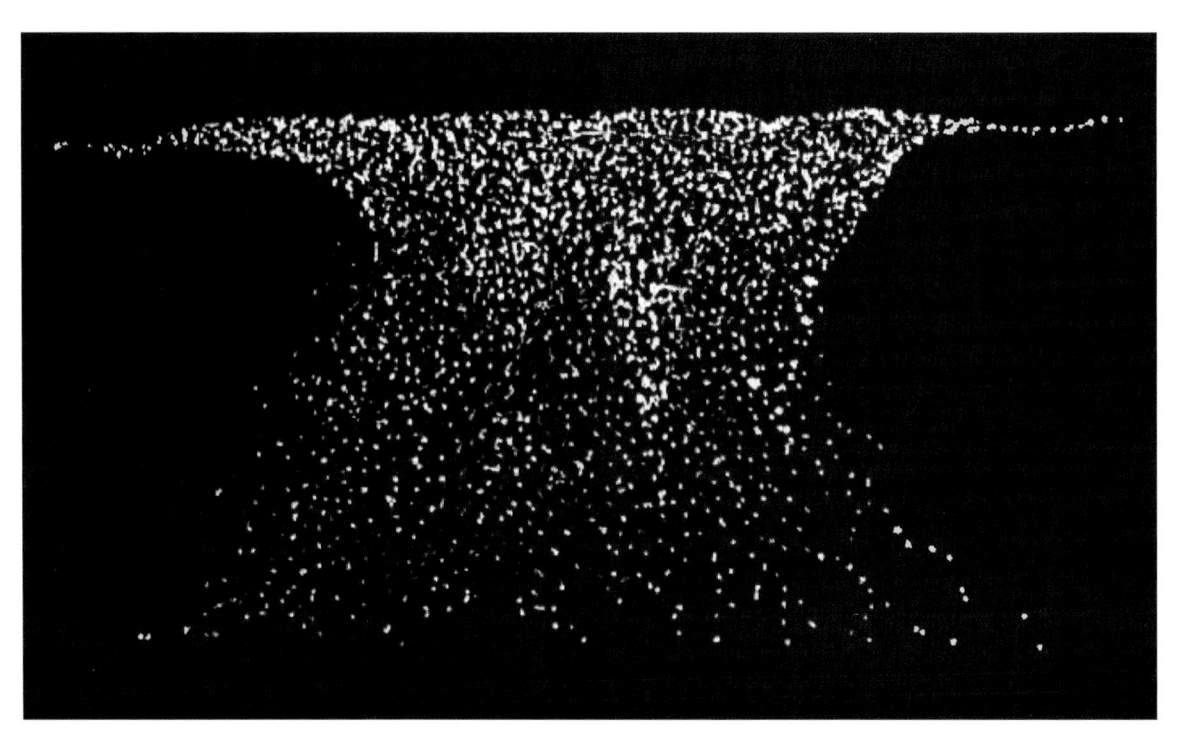

Operative drawings #21. I further simplified the drawings down to spots and dots organized as roads and corridors. These were less easy to perceive once projected in space but could still be seen and followed.

Operative drawing #25. Only drawing white pixels now, I digitally arranged them in geometric structures, wondering how a body would travel in space according to such forms when projected.

Video still of performative prototyping with operative drawing #25. Once this drawing was projected, I could perceive parts of the geometry inherent to the drawing but these were distorted by my body moving through them, leading me to travel in space via constant twists and turns. At this point, I was fascinated by the movement of the projected pixels shifting according to the uneven surface of my body. As soon as I stopped moving, all the pixels covering my body would freeze. I started considering the possibility of a projected beam of light that would only appear on and as the body moved, whereby stillness would trigger darkness.

starting to move in fragmentary ways that felt, at first, very odd, as if my body was a puppet manipulated by someone else.

Progressively, what first felt like tip-toeing from one unusual movement to another became more fluid and less hesitant to the point of feeling the projection on my body as if it were clothed in the projected motifs. By this point, the performative prototyping of these drawings offered a most unexpected visual phenomenon, perceivable both from within and from without: my body's movement seemed to trigger the projected content to move. When standing still within the field of light, the white particles imprinted on my body were quite simply static. Any vibration of my body would make them vibrate too. The projections would be animated as I moved and I could control, to some extent, their alterations according to my movements. Further, even when still, any sudden and tiny movement of light would make me aware of the inconsistency of my stillness, thereby requiring greater efforts to remain static. And these were as unusual to my body as much of the stronger movements I was trying out. In both cases, I was compelled to become aware of every part and limb of my body and to input similar precision and control to articulate each and every body part.

Swimming in the dark pools of the projections' glowing particles, my body seemed no longer a cohesive, singular and autonomous entity, but a fragmentary, multiple and dependent structure, whose every movement was impelled by the outside: the rather extreme proximity of this outside substituted for any internal instigation of movement. Between stillness and motion, I discovered a palette of sometimes difficult slow motions that I had not experienced before. The scope of movement in the projected content was determined by my body's movement. But since the projected content was inherently static and always present in space, I could only alter it to some extent: for instance, I could not, by way of moving, make the projected motifs disappear, or appear, or shift their location in space, or overlap them. However, these more drastic visual phenomena thus became of interest to me as a way to further expand the potential for physical interaction.

ADVANCED PRACTICE

The digital projection of the static drawings I had produced led to a particular point in the inquiry where the body's moving presence in the projection compelled its content to move on the body's surface. I concluded this phase by speculating about a more dynamic and interactive kind of projection/light whose occurrence and movement would hinge entirely on the body's presence and movement. In other words, I sought to know whether the previously observed relation between body and light could be expanded in such a way that even the appearance and disappearance of projection would be based on the live body's movement. This meant that the digital nature of the medium (projector and computer) would need to be more profoundly utilized: the slideshow software I had been using to project the drawings needed to be replaced by new software that could activate and animate projected content according to the movements of the body. Although there is existing software with these kinds of function, I was keen to engage in the process of developing new software from scratch. This was mostly due to the fact that I did not want an existing software's framework to limit the scope of the research as much as it occurred previously with the commercial slideshow software.

Thus, this new phase of the research was driven by the creation of custom-made software. However, creating software requires digital programming, which is not an area of expertise of mine. Therefore, I turned to digital programmers and developers to discuss the fundamental conditions and intentions that had been previously developed as a framework for creating bespoke software. From the onset of these discussions it became apparent that digital programmers working with interactive systems are customarily used to interactions being triggered by hands and fingers touching a screen, a surface or an object. As a result, the requirement for the volume of space (including the entire body within it) to become the sensitive areas of interaction was troubling yet interesting to programmers. I thus decided to draw a sketch that would include tactile elements that programmers were used to but that could also be understood without these elements.

Interactive Scenario is an operative drawing presenting key operational concepts at stake in the research, applied to common understandings of touch-triggered interactivity. The drawing shows bodies placing their hands against a screen, resulting in a small beam of light appearing right

Operative drawing *Interactive Scenario*. This drawing was made to communicate to a digital programmer the kind of interaction I was interested in developing: as hands touch and travel on the surface of a screen, light would appear on the hands and follow them. However, I wanted this to happen without a screen or any material device, so as to interact with the air as I had experienced in my previous experiments.

next to their hands. At the same time, the sketch is also suggestive of the same phenomenon without a screen to touch: the projected light comes from behind the screen, traversing it and continuing throughout the volume of space until it reaches the floor in front of the screen, where the bodies are located. To re-imagine this scenario without the screen, whereby the movement of the hand and of the whole body alone would trigger the appearance of projection/light on the body itself, would initiate the kind of interactive phenomenon I was pursuing. Furthermore, the drawing suggests that, as the hand moves across the screen's surface, the light beam follows and grows. This upsizing of the projection/light was envisioned as an autonomous occurrence, independent from the body's kinesis, so as to provide additional and unpredictable stimuli to which the body could physically respond. After presenting and explaining this sketch to digital programmers, it became apparent that the main challenge was going to be related to finding a way for the software to perceive the body's motion in a pitch-black space, so as to trigger projection. Evidently, a volume of space is immaterial, unlike the physical surface of a screen. So, to perceive and react to the body's movement in space, the volume of space and the body needed to be approached altogether as one screen. But how could the spatial volume's lack of material substance be perceived, or tracked, alongside movement in the dark?

Although a volume of space appears to lack substance to the human eye, air is actually filled with particles of various types. In particular, air can

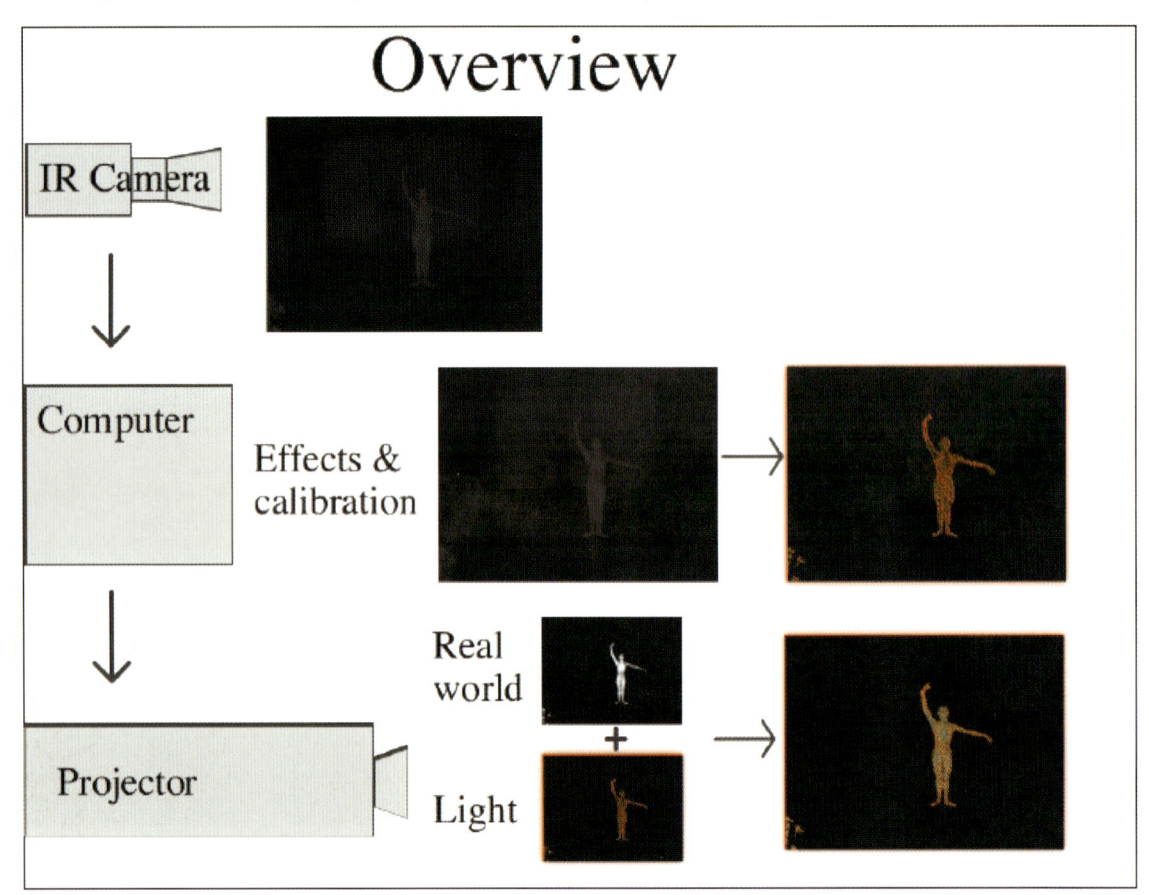

Schematic overview of interactive projection system by Robin Beitra. This is a schematic representation of the hardware system put in place around the bespoke software developed to produce the interactive lighting I had come to speculate about.

be filled with wavelengths of light that, although invisible to our eyes, are nonetheless affected by our moving bodies. Infrared light has wavelengths that cannot be perceived by human vision, yet they are disturbed and temporarily altered when a body moves through it. Infrared cameras are devices that filter out all the wavelengths of the light spectrum except infrared. In this way, these cameras can perceive infrared lighting, especially when it is disturbed and altered by a moving object (essentially the movement of the object displaces part of the infrared wavelength forcing it to accumulate in density and thus become more visually explicit to the infrared camera).

So, the development of the custom-made software started with the programming of a digital base, an algorithmic skeleton, which interfaced the fundamental relations needed between different pieces of hardware. To put it simply, an infrared camera needed to relay what it captured to a computer where the software would analyse any discrepancy in the infrared wavelengths (resulting from moving objects) picked up by the camera, in order to communicate to the projector whether any action was needed.

One of the challenges working with infrared light is found in the way that many sources of light comprise of the infrared wavelengths (including sunlight). In order for the infrared camera to perceive the alteration of infrared wavelengths as a result of moving objects, the environment under the camera's observation must have an even spread of infrared light. Any moving body or object that will then disturb the homogeneity of the infrared spread will trigger projection where the disturbance is occurring. This means that the environment's lighting conditions must be controlled: infrared sources of light must be used and positioned in such a way as to spread evenly the wavelengths across the spatial volume. If there is any other additional lighting in the space, this can disturb the spread of infrared wavelengths. To remedy this issue, the space must be either pitch black or the infrared sources of light must be superior in power to the other lights that are emitting some infrared wavelength.

The digital base of the software essentially structured the primary asset of the software: projection appears when, where and for as long as movement occurs. This digital programming required experimentation in real space to calibrate the timely simultaneity and precise spatial overlap of live movement and projection. Interestingly, during these experiments, whilst the programmer, Robin Beitra, was calibrating the precision of the software's interactivity in time and space, my body also found itself adapting to this surprisingly more confounding phenomenon. At the start of these experiments, my body had to learn to slow down again as any movement would immediately trigger projection, even the mildest shifts occurring within the fabric of the T-shirt I was wearing would impel small white shards of light to appear. The stillness of the entire body that was required to prevent a response from the projector and maintain a state of darkness was very difficult to achieve. At first, whenever I was attempting to be still, light would appear and show me areas of my body that were still moving, or rather vibrating. Those were usually small areas on my body, to which I would normally not pay much attention. Their movement was coming from within my organs: lungs but also visceral activities. To be still meant to calm the internal activity down, as well as all segments of my body's surface. Effectively, the stillness that would trigger complete black-out was the most physically testing: a restless state of stillness. Opposite to the stillness of relaxation, it is the kind of stillness that Andre Lepecki (2004) links to exhaustion and disappearance as expanded modes of perception: 'stillness-in-motion [enables] shifting the limits of our senses of time and space' (Lepecki 2004: 141). As I was gradually able to stay still without any projected light occurring, an unusual sense of space was emerging: a simultaneous awareness of the inside and outside of my body, which involved the sensation of a dissolve of the border (my skin).

Now that my whole body had found an effective physical relation to the interactive projection, I could explore specific and isolated movements. There again, when trying solely to move my left arm, it appeared that the rest of my body was moving too, since light occurred everywhere on me. Thus, in order to develop some control over the light's responsiveness, I rapidly stopped moving in the everyday ways I am accustomed to (just like I had to change my usual way of being still). Instead, I would repeat a simple gesture again and again, reducing it and slowing it down in order to ensure that only one arm was moving and thus illuminated. This involved keeping an awareness of my body's predominantly contrived stillness, while paying attention to how my arm moved or stopped moving. When such precise and dual awareness and control of all body parts was achieved, and the digital calibration of the software was completed, the projected light I was triggering would become somehow controllable, almost graspable. As my body had adapted to the situation, the lighting phenomena triggered by the interactive system could now be further detailed, thereby testing my body's adaptation further.

The visual effects of the projection/light itself were thus the next detailed assets of the software to be programmed. It is in this asset that the key perceptual qualities of the light were evolved. Up until that point, the projected content was just white light. In order to give it other colours, textures, forms and behaviours, these basic properties were again tried out and refined through practical experimentation in a black box. In this case, simply moving my body could not be sufficient to trigger effects in the projection, since this was already the basic condition for the projection to simply appear. Thus, physical movements had to be further specified in relation to particular effects. For instance, fast and abrupt movements could change the projected light's colour or vertical movements (jumps) could modify the direction of the light's movement.

But requiring light to behave in such different ways meant that the behaviour of this digitally engineered lighting could not simply replicate the real behaviours of light's propagation. We thus considered the algorithmic translations of different types of natural phenomena to diversify the light's behaviour. For instance, we introduced the behavioural properties of clouds into the software to provide it with trailing effects. A projected spot of light could appear on a moving hand, which, as it was moved around, would leave a luminous trail behind or would take a completely new direction. These trailing effects complicated the visual phenomena and, accordingly, required a far more complex set of physical movements to trigger them. The body required for these experiments needed to be able to perform a wide array of precisely controlled movements, albeit to be a highly trained body. Thus, a dancer, Laura Doehler, was invited to take my body's place, and the software was further programmed with a variety of interactive effects. Unsurprisingly, Laura was quickly able to interact with the light and evolve a complex physical relationship with it. In doing so, she made much use of her movement training, yet she also needed to adapt her movement abilities and qualities. As I had discovered with my body in the previous experiments, the dancer also found herself having to move more slowly and incrementally to separate and activate different body parts.

At this point, the software was sufficiently elaborate to be consolidated, shared and used in front of the public. However, implementing this system for the first time within a performance production was risky, simply due to the fact that such productions have a range of other design and performative components all tied up together. Therefore, any issue with a new tool like this one could generate problems for other aspects of the production, which could be generally detrimental to it. It was thus safer to present this interactive system first on its own. For this reason, it was first presented as a self-contained immersive installation titled Wearable Shadows at the Kinetica ArtFair (2011). There, we built a small black box whose only source of light was a digital projector connected to our interactive projection system

Video still of performative prototyping with dancer. In order to develop the software for the interactive lighting system, many experiments with bodies were undertaken in black box studios with all the relevant hardware. Initially, my body was used for testing but as the interactive lighting became more nuanced, the body needed to have a broader and more detailed vocabulary of movement, thus a dancer replaced me.

(hardware and software). As such, if no audience was present or moving in the space, complete darkness reigned. As soon as a body entered and moved around, light was projected on and around the body. A diverse range of bodies visited the space, and it was fascinating to discover the range of reactions and interactions: from teenagers lacking the attention or patience to realize that something was going on in the room, to older people who would spend much time gently interacting with the projected light as if knitting luminous and transparent objects suspended in the air. Yet again, a few dancers visited the room and interacted most creatively with the light, thereby confirming that the system was ready for performance productions. Since then, I have used this system to design multiple dance productions in small and large venues, in the UK and abroad. For each of these performances, new lighting phenomena and effects have been integrated into the software making it ever more complex and, in return, invoking to various degrees different kinetic physicality on the part of the dancers. As such, this research continues, not within the laboratory context of the prototyping phases but within professional contexts of production.

Wearable Shadows, installation at Kinetica ArtFair 2011, created by the author in collaboration with Daniel Felstead. Once the interactive lighting system was well developed, and before applying it to performance productions, it was presented on its own as an immersive and interactive installation. In this way, the system's robustness over time was tested. It was also fascinating to see how a diverse range of bodies experienced it differently. Here, the photograph captures (in long exposure) a dancer who spent some time interacting with the installation by herself. This confirmed the system was ready to be applied to performance productions. DANIEL FELSTEAD

PROFESSIONAL INSIGHT

MEASURING
Oren Sagiv

Oren Sagiv is Professor of Architecture at Bezalel Academy of Art and Design in Jerusalem. In 2004, he founded Studio Oren Sagiv, which focuses on architectural installations for the world's leading museums, galleries and cultural events and festivals, as well as for dance, theatre and performance. The studio is active in designing unique ephemeral structures reacting on specific urban situations and thus exploring and investigating possible forms in the city's fabric.

We ponder, reflect, wish, consent and oppose, doubt or make fierce statements about, and toward, the world around us through words – words we say and words we write. However, when we start to make meaning through objects we make, it is the very first moment of a revolution.

Consider introducing yourself to others through an object you are to construct only for this purpose. Such introduction, unlike the common one, is not a story told with words, it is not historical but physical and the object has to be able to contain an inherent meaning that can replace words. One, perhaps more common, way of going about this task is to create an object that represents, to your own subjective belief, one or more qualities that characterize you: materials, forms and colours can be seen to be appropriate to tell your story. But such an object is illustrative whereby representation is primary. Differently, this exercise is an opportunity to explore mediation as a new way of thinking and acting, one in which the inherent value in what you make is the objective end.

We may see this process as an act of measuring, in which one crucial starting point is to remember that, initially, a measure is not a standardized number or a value, but is directly connected to a physical object (i.e. 'measuring' is a verb leading to the creation of 'a measure', which is a noun). To assist you in defining how and what you will measure, you should select one guiding term. Examining your body like a structure, you should choose terms pertaining to spatial and material properties – like 'balance', 'proportion', 'tension', 'intensity', 'stability', 'joint', 'border' or 'envelope'. But what could be the procedure of

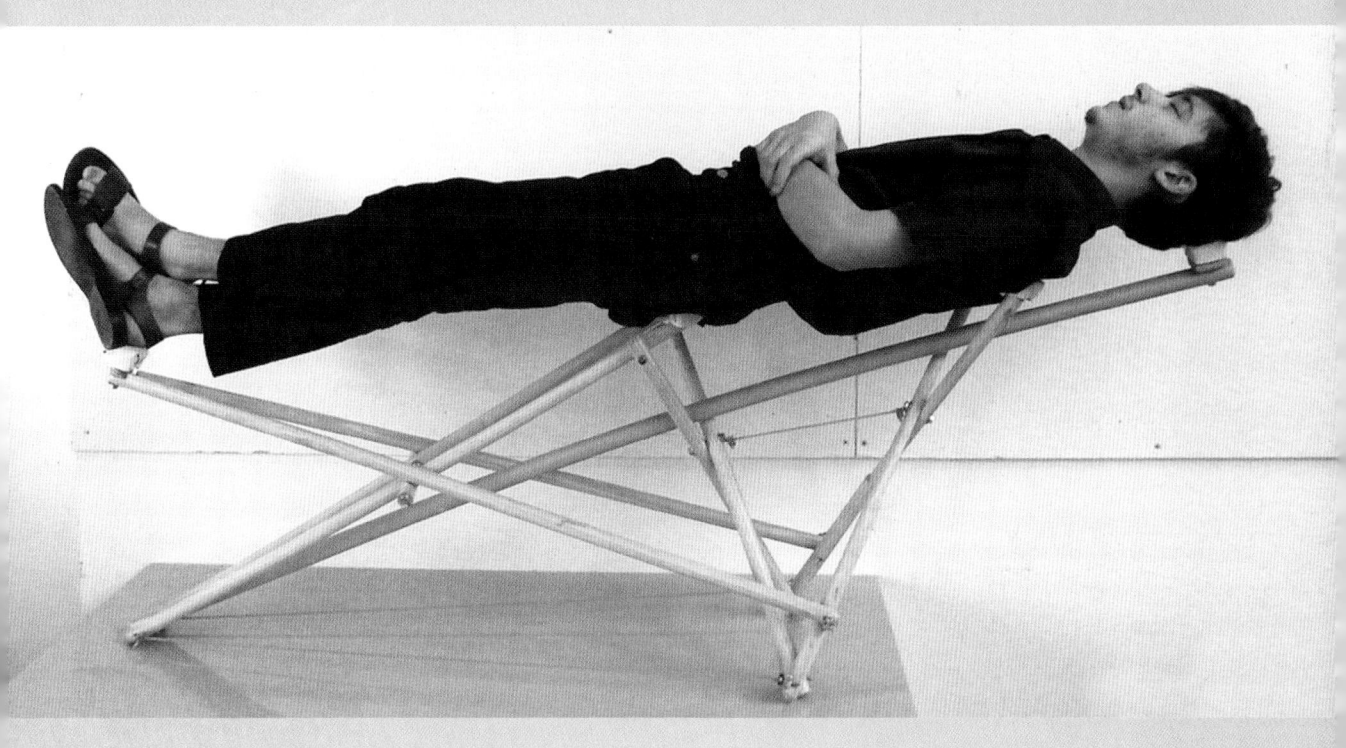

Edge by Simon Krantz, Daniel Rauchwerger and Joel Rubinstein. BEZALEL ACADEMY OF ARTS AND DESIGN, ARCHITECTURE DEPARTMENT

(*continued overleaf*)

(*continued from previous page*)

Envelope by Yael Era Pano and Elena Kosse. BEZALEL ACADEMY OF ARTS AND DESIGN, ARCHITECTURE DEPARTMENT

measuring 'proportion', 'stability' or 'border' on one's body? What could possibly be the measuring instrument and what could a result of such measuring look like?

The term you choose serves as the conceptual dimension – an intellectual periphery, which encompasses a web of textual meanings. It can help direct you towards an intention that will inform your actions, trials and physical procedures that follow. In parallel, questions arise as to what is it exactly, in relation to the term we choose, we want to measure in the body. In other words, what do you direct your actions to and what do you ignore? This decision is bound to be answered with wisdom and imagination and it is dependent on another question, that of how do you measure; in other words, what kind of procedure can you come up with and use?

If your starting point is the term envelope, a straightforward possibility could be to create an object that mediates the area of your skin. You may consider the material procedures relevant to dealing with different challenges: which material is strong and flexible enough to be able to wrap with preciseness around the tiniest space, such as between fingers or behind ears? At the same time, the act of enveloping evokes the concept of 'developing' – as an agency to reveal the structure of a three-dimensional form by reducing it to a surface. You would, therefore, find yourself committing to the procedure of folding and unfolding, looking for the optimal relations between the complex form you measure and the form of the two-dimensional final result.

If your starting point is the term edge, you may start by looking for different ways to register the edges of your body (amongst a multitude of other possible interpretative resonances existing between the term 'edge' and the body). Your efforts may lead you to designing a structure that is uniquely tailored to, and activated by, your own bodily edges. Such a structure could, for instance, touch on, and extend on, a minimal number of points of your body to elevate it above the ground and stabilize it by dispersing your body weight via a minimal amount of points on the floor. The object would precisely mediate a measure of your body by corresponding to your body's specific weight, structure and dimensions – supporting your body and, at the same time, obtaining rigidity and stability by it. Needless to say, only your body could use this object; the success or failure of the measuring is clear – were you accurate enough in your intention, design and execution – will the measure you have created work or fail?

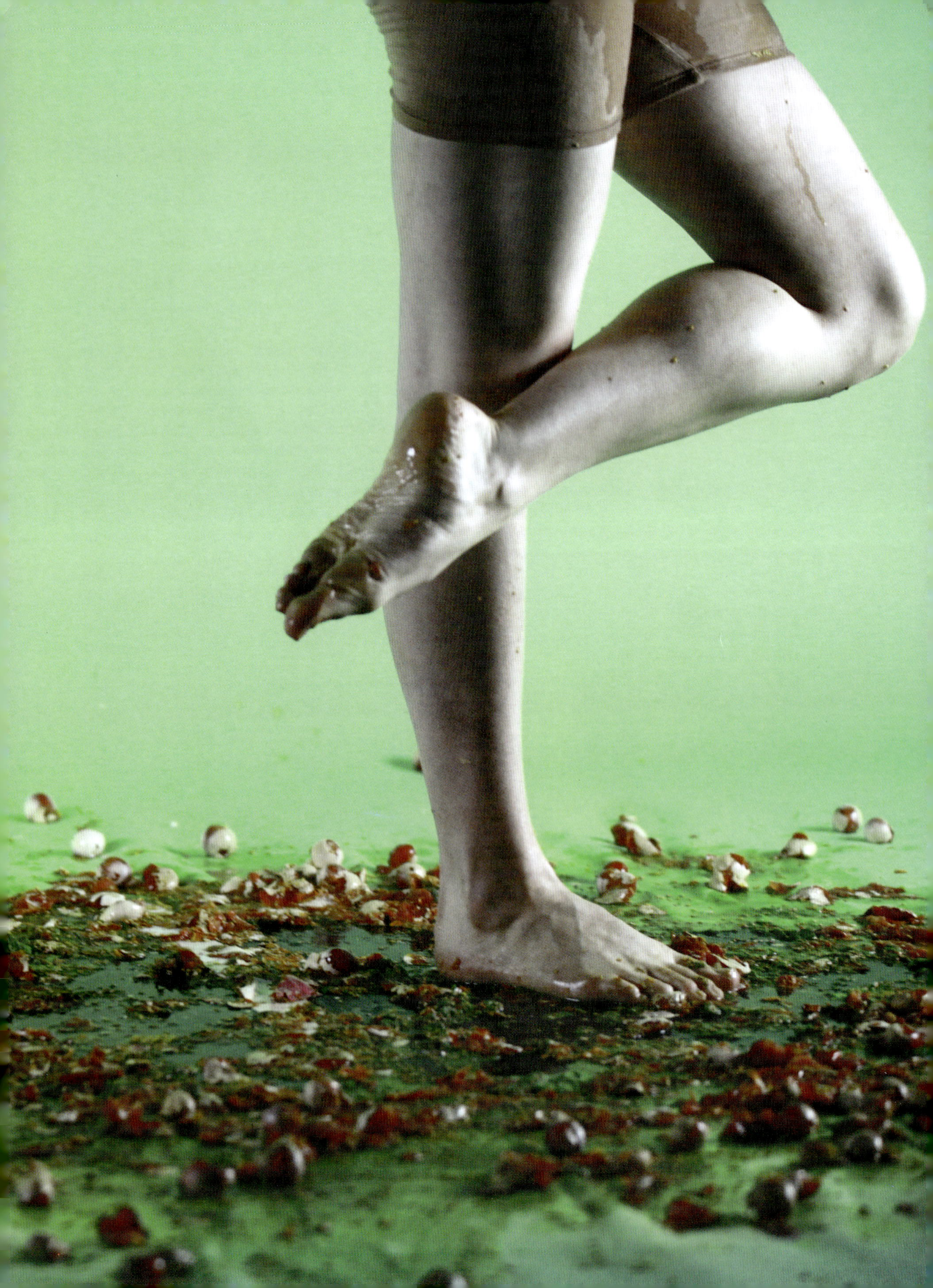

CONCLUSION

The live body is at the heart of scenography. Indeed, performance scholars have written much about the primacy of the presence of the actor (States 1987; Fischer-Lichte 1997; McAuley 2000; Howard 2002; Baugh 2005). Scenography is, then, understood as a form of interdisciplinarity, which 'seamless synthesis' (Howard 2002: xx) hinges on the 'centrality of the actors' (McAuley 2000: 282) who are deemed to be 'dynamic agent[s] responsible for energizing the performance space [,] endowing it with meaning and drawing meaning from it' (McAuley 2000: 282). In this model, the body of the audience is another pivotal point wherein scenography would be 'the measured space of […] a meeting point between actors and a potential audience' (Howard 2002: 1), i.e. a 'given space' for 'the interaction between performers and spectators' (McAuley 2000: 5). Thus, when devoid of bodies, the scenographic space would be 'silent, empty and inert' (Howard 2002: 1).

These predominant ideas about scenography imply particular conceptions of the body and space. The body is presumed to have a kind of superiority over space, since without it the space would have nothing to communicate, no dynamic life of its own. Accordingly, space is 'measured' or 'given', which is to say that it is simply granted the subaltern status of being the product of the human intellect. It is easy to detect here how scenography can function as a metaphor of the classical ideology of human 'mastery over the environment' (Lakoff and Johnson 2003: 229).

OPPOSITE: *Prosthetic Gods* by Dallas Wexler. JEMIMA YONG

Though traditional in scenography, this conception of space as a mere backdrop to showcasing human control is problematic in light of the disastrous effects of human presence on the environment. Do we humans really energize the environments we inhabit? The emphasis on the human body in scenography is certainly an opportunity to ask such question and problematize our position in, and relation to, the world. Yet, at the same time, the scenographic focus on space's relation to the body is precisely an opportunity to explore and propose new and more sustainable ways of inhabiting the earth.

A century ago, Adolphe Appia wished to explore the potential for scenography to be 'inspired by the human body' (Beacham 1993: 110): a body that is not entangled in a *mind over matter* ideology but that precisely recognizes a productive threshold where matter is a constituent of, and thus equal to, the human mind. This implies re-empowering the material presence of the environment on stage, and thus re-envisioning the position of the human body in a balanced relationship with the spaces and beings surrounding it, therein advancing a 'new social practice' (Appia in Beacham 1993: 109).

This is especially critical given that most creative practices of a scenographic kind are involved in entertainment industries, which generate a vast amount of waste. As designers of temporary environments, situations and events, we often mobilize directly or indirectly quantities of materials and substances, some more toxic than others, but most of which are eventually trashed.

Remnants by Leanne Vandenbussche. A reconstruction of a previously destroyed scale model of Richard Wagner's *Festspielhaus* in Bayreuth. JEMIMA YONG

Whilst we can explore new imaginative and sustainable modes of dwelling that are physically and aesthetically expressed, there is also a need for revising the material procedures and outcomes by which we undertake and effectively present these explorations. Although our audiences, and often even ourselves, do not see all the waste resulting from our work, our critical awareness and engagement with this hidden dimension of scenography is an ethical imperative.

BIBLIOGRAPHY

Albertová, H. (2008) *Josef Svoboda: Scenographer*. Prague: Divadelní Ústave.

Baugh, C. (2005) *Theatre, Performance and Technology*. London: Palgrave MacMillan.

Beacham, R. C., ed. (1993) *Adolphe Appia: Texts on Theatre*. London and New York: Routledge.

Bogart, A. and Landau, T. (2005) *The Viewpoints Book. A Practical Guide to Viewpoints and Composition*. New York: Theatre Communications Group New York.

Bradby, D. (2006) *Theatre of Movement and Gesture*. London and New York: Routledge.

Brook, P. (1968) *The Empty Space. A Book About the Theatre: Deadly, Holy, Rough, Immediate*. New York: Atheneum.

Butterworth, P. (2005) *Magic on the Early English Stage*. Cambridge: Cambridge University Press.

Collins, J. and Nisbet, A., eds (2010) *Theatre and Performance Design. A Reader in Scenography*. London and New York: Routledge.

Crary, J. (2001) *Suspensions of Perception: Attention, Spectacle and Modern Culture*. Cambridge, Mass.: MIT Press.

Epstein, J. (1970) *The Black Box Group: An Experiment in Visual Theatre*. London: Latimer Press.

Fischer-Lichte, E. (1997) *The Show and the Gaze of Theatre: A European Perspective*. Translated by J. Riley. Iowa City: University of Iowa Press.

Foreman, R. (1992) *Unbalancing Acts: Foundations for a Theater*. New York: TCG.

Garelick, R. (2007) *Electric Salome: Loie Fuller's Performance of Modernism*. Princeton: Princeton University Press.

Garner, S. (1994) *Bodied Spaces: Phenomenology and Performance in Contemporary Theatre*. Ithaca, NV and London: Cornell University Press.

Giesekam, G. (2007) *Staging the Screen*. New York: Palgrave Macmillan.

Gropius, W. and Wensinger, A. S., eds (1961) *The Theater of the Bauhaus*. Translated by A. S. Wensinger. Baltimore, Md: John Hopkins University Press.

Howard, P. (2002) *What is Scenography?* London and New York: Routledge.

Ingold, T. (2011) *Being Alive: Essays on Movement, Knowledge and Description*. London and New York: Routledge.

Innes, C. (1998) *Edward Gordon Craig: A Vision of Theatre*. London and New York: Routledge.

Lakoff, G. and Johnson, M. (2003) *Metaphors We Live By*. Chicago: University Of Chicago Press.

Lehmann, H.-T. (2006) *Postdramatic Theatre*. London and New York: Routledge.

Lepecki, A. (2004) *Of the Presence of the Body*. Middletown: Wesleyan University Press.

McAuley, G. (2000) *Space in Performance: Making Meaning in the Theatre*. Ann Arbor: The University of Michigan Press.

McKinney, J. and Butterworth, P. (2009) *The Cambridge Introduction to Scenography*. Cambridge: Cambridge University Press.

Newlove, J. and Dalby, J. (2005) *Laban for All*. London: Nick Hern Books.

Oliveros, P. (1971) 'Sonic Meditations' in Austin, L. & Kahn, D. eds (2011) *Source: Music of the Avant-Garde 1966-1973*. Berkeley, Los Angeles, London: University of California Press. pp.342–345

Oliveros, P. (2010) Lawton Hall, ed. *Sounding the Margins: Collected Writings 1992–2009*. Kingston, New York: Deep Listening Publications.

Omlin, S. (2014) *Smokey Pokership: Perform the Exhibition Space*. Nürnberg: Verlag für Moderne Kunst.

Pavelka, M. (2015) *So You Want to be a Theatre Designer?* London: Nick Hern Books.

Perec, G. (2008) *Species of Spaces and Other Pieces*. Harmondsworth: Penguin Classics.

Read, A. (1995) *Theatre and Everyday Life: An Ethics of Performance*. London and New York: Routledge.

Robertson, L. (2003) *Seven Walks From The Office For Soft Architecture*. Astoria: Clear Cut Press.

Salter, C. (2010) *Entangled: Technology and the Transformation of Performance*. Cambridge, Mass.: MIT Press.

Schön, D. A. (1983) *The Reflective Practitioner: How Professionals Think in Action*. New York: Basic Books.

States, B. O. (1987) *Great Reckonings in Little Rooms: On the Phenomenology of Theater*. Berkeley: University of California Press.

Warner, M. (2006) *Phantasmagoria*. Oxford: Oxford University Press.

Wiles, D. (2003) *A Short History of Western Performance Space*. Cambridge: Cambridge University Press.

INDEX

Page numbers in *italics* indicate images and diagrams; those in **bold** indicate guidance and practical recommendations.

3-D see three dimensional representation
abstraction, in composition 90, *90*, *91*
additive colours 97
aerial viewpoints 16, 21, *22–23*, 39
  see also ground plans
aesthetic aspects, prototyping 78
aperture of lens **122**
Appia, Adolphe 12, 155
artefacts
  digital design 55
  fragmentation and branching 92–93, *93*
  mock-ups 67–68, *68*
  testing **74**
assembly plans 113, *114*, 115, *115*
asymmetry, for contrast 100, *101*
audience
  diverse reactions to installations 149
  as participants 132, *132*
  relationship with **105–107**
audience awareness in composition **105–107**
  see also viewpoints
axonometric rendering 115, *115*

Bauhaus performance 136
black box projection project 130–150
  dramaturgical approach 130
  speculative drawing conceptualisation 131–136, *131*, *132*, *133*, *134*, *135*
  operative drawing *137*, *138–139*, 139–144, *141–143*, 146
  digital software development 144–149, *145*, *146*
  installation stage 148–149, *150*
black box theatre 129, 130
blocking (operative drawing) 21
bodies
  bodily dimension principle 7–8
  conceptualisation through measurement 151, **151–153**, *152–153*
  as negative space 129–130
  role in prototyping **74**, 140–149, *143*, *149*
  role in scenography 155
body dimension, principle of scenography 7–8
body 'measuring' **151–153**
Bogart, Anne 8, 43, 45, 71
branching (composition) 92–93, *93*

cameras, manual settings **122, 125**
character rendering 15
  see also costume, costume rendering
chiaroscuro 101
chromostereopsis see stereoptic depth perception
chronological ordering (portfolios) 117
circles, drawing *58–59*, **58**
CMYK subtractive colours 97
collaboration see communication for collaboration

colour
  in composition 97–100, *98–99*, *98*, *99*, 102
  cultural symbolism 100
  in models 51, *52–53*, 55, **63**
  in projected light 148
communication for collaboration
  see also dialogue
  dialogic principle 8, **8**
  role of documentation 109
  role of drawing 23, 29
  role of models 33
  role of prototyping 67, **85**
complementary colours, effects 99
composition
  audience awareness **105–107**
  colours in composition 97–100, *98–99*, *98*, *99*, 102
  contemporary 92–95, *93*, *94*, *95*
  contrast in composition 99–100, 100–102, *101*, *102*, *103*
  modernist 89–92, *89*, *90*, *91*
  movement trajectories 95–97, **96**
  in photography **127**
  traditional 87–89, *88*
  visual narrative 102–104, *104*
concealed frameworks 129
conceptual frameworks, in prototyping 71–73, *72*
conceptualisation
  see also speculative drawing
  and audience awareness **105**